First World War
and Army of Occupation
War Diary
France, Belgium and Germany

56 DIVISION
Headquarters, Branches and Services
Royal Army Veterinary Corps
Assistant Director Veterinary Services
16 October 1915 - 30 April 1919

WO95/2939/3

The Naval & Military Press Ltd
www.nmarchive.com
Published in association with The National Archives

Published by

The Naval & Military Press Ltd

Unit 10 Ridgewood Industrial Park,

Uckfield, East Sussex,

TN22 5QE England

Tel: +44 (0) 1825 749494

www.naval-military-press.com

www.nmarchive.com

This diary has been reprinted in facsimile from the original. Any imperfections are inevitably reproduced and the quality may fall short of modern type and cartographic standards.

© Crown Copyright
Images reproduced by permission of The National Archives, London, England, 2015.

Contents

Document type	Place/Title	Date From	Date To
Heading	WO95/2939-3		
Heading	56th Division Asst Dir. Vety Service Mar 1916-Apr 1919		
Heading	War Diary of A.D.V.S,, 56th (London) Division. From March 1st-1916 To March 31st 1916 Vol II		
Heading	ADVS 56 Div Vol III		
War Diary	Domart	01/03/1916	12/03/1916
War Diary	Doullens	12/03/1916	31/03/1916
War Diary	Le Cauroy	01/04/1916	30/04/1916
War Diary	Henu Map Lens II	05/05/1916	31/05/1916
War Diary	Henu	02/06/1916	30/06/1916
War Diary		28/06/1916	28/06/1916
War Diary	Henu	01/07/1916	28/08/1916
War Diary	Doullens	21/08/1916	21/08/1916
War Diary	Frohen Le Grand	22/08/1916	22/08/1916
War Diary	St Riquier	23/08/1916	31/08/1916
Heading	War Diary of A.D.V.S., 56th (London) Division From September 1st 1916 To September 30th 1916 Vol 7		
War Diary	St Riquier	01/09/1916	04/09/1916
War Diary	Corbie	05/09/1916	06/09/1916
War Diary	L2 b 1.1 Stat 62D	07/09/1916	07/09/1916
War Diary	F 21 b Sheet 62 D	07/09/1916	14/09/1916
War Diary	F 24 C Central Sheet 62D	15/09/1916	21/09/1916
War Diary	F 21 b 55 Sheet 62 D	22/09/1916	29/09/1916
War Diary	War Diary Of A.D.V.S. 56th (London) Division From October 1st 1916 To October 31st 1916. Vol 8		
War Diary	F 21 b 55 Sheet 62 D	01/10/1916	01/10/1916
War Diary	A3C03 Sheet 62 C	02/10/1916	10/10/1916
War Diary	F 21 b 55 Sheet 62D	11/10/1916	11/10/1916
War Diary	Belloy Sur Somme	12/10/1916	18/10/1916
War Diary	Hallencourt	20/10/1916	24/10/1916
War Diary	Lestrem	25/10/1916	27/10/1916
War Diary	Lestrem Sheet 36 A	28/10/1916	28/10/1916
War Diary	La Gorgue Sheet 36A	30/10/1916	31/10/1916
War Diary	La Gorgue L34 Sheet 36 A	01/11/1916	30/11/1916
Heading	War Diary of A.D.V.S. 56th (London) Division From December 1st 1916 To December 31st 1916 Vol 10		
War Diary	La Gorgue L 34 Sheet 36A	01/12/1916	31/12/1916
Heading	War Diary of A.D.V.S. 56th (London) Division From January 1st 1917 To January 31st 1917 Vol XI		
War Diary	La Gorgue L34 Sheet 36 A	01/01/1917	31/01/1917
Heading	War Diary of A.D.V.S. 56th (London) Division From February 1-1917 To February 28th-1917 Vol 12		
War Diary	La Gorgue L34 Sheet 36A	02/02/1917	28/02/1917
War Diary	War Diary of A.D.V.S. 56th (London) Division From March 1st 1917 To March 31st 1917 Vol 13		
War Diary	La Gorgue L 34 Sheet 36 A	01/03/1917	03/03/1917
War Diary	Wail Lens II Le Cauroy	05/03/1917	21/03/1917
War Diary	Beaumetz Les Loges Sheet 51 C Q 23	23/03/1917	31/03/1917

Heading	War Diary of A.D.V.S. 56th Division From April 1st 1917 To April 30th 1917 Vol 14		
War Diary	Beaumetz Les Loges Sheet 51 C Q23	01/04/1917	13/04/1917
War Diary	Achicourt Sheet 51 B M 2 b 14	13/04/1917	17/04/1917
War Diary	Couin Sheet 57D J 1	19/04/1917	24/04/1917
War Diary	Hauteville Sheet 51C J 35	24/04/1917	27/04/1917
War Diary	Arras Sheet 51 B 921	29/04/1917	29/04/1917
Heading	War Diary of A.D.V.S. 56th Division From May 1st 1917 To May 31st 1917 Vol 15		
War Diary	Arras Sheet 51 B G 21	01/05/1917	19/05/1917
War Diary	Warlus Sheet 51B	23/05/1917	23/05/1917
War Diary	Habarc	25/05/1917	30/05/1917
Heading	War Diary of A.D.V.S. 56th Division From June 1st 1917 To June 30th 1917 Vol 16		
War Diary	Habarc Sheet 57 C K8	01/06/1917	08/06/1917
War Diary	Arras Sheet 51B G 21	09/06/1917	29/06/1917
Heading	War Diary of A.D.V.S. 56th Division From July 1st 1917 To July 31st 1917 Vol 17		
War Diary	Arras Sheet 51B G 21	02/07/1917	02/07/1917
War Diary	Le Cauroy Lens II	04/07/1917	21/07/1917
War Diary	Eperlecques	23/07/1917	23/07/1917
War Diary	Hazebrouck 5 A	26/07/1917	28/07/1917
Heading	War Diary of D.A.D.V.S. 56th (London) Division From August 1-1917 To August 31-1917 Vol 18		
War Diary	Eperlecques	02/08/1917	02/08/1917
War Diary	Hazebrouck 5A	02/08/1917	03/08/1917
War Diary	Reninghelst Sheet 28 G.28.b.4d	06/08/1917	22/08/1917
War Diary	Eperlecques	23/08/1917	23/08/1917
War Diary	Hazebrouk 5 A	23/08/1917	30/08/1917
War Diary	Fremicourt Lens II K 5	30/08/1917	31/08/1917
Heading	War Diary Of D.A.D.V.S. 56th Division From Sept 1st 1917 To 30th 1917 Vol 19		
War Diary	Fremicourt Lens II K 5	01/09/1917	29/09/1917
Heading	War Diary of D.A.D.V.S. 56th Division From October 1st 1917 To October 31st 1917 Vol 20		
War Diary	Fremicourt Lens XI K 5	01/10/1917	28/10/1917
Heading	War Diary of D.A.D.V.S. 56th Division From Nov 1st 1917 To Nov. 31st 1917 Vol 21		
War Diary	Fremicourt Sheet Lens 11, Square K5.	01/11/1917	29/11/1917
Heading	War Diary of D.A.D.V.S. 56th (London) Division From December 1st 17 To December 31st 17 Vol 22		
War Diary	Fremicourt Sheet Lens II Sq K 5	01/12/1917	03/12/1917
War Diary	Sheet Lens II Sq 9 Fosseaux	03/12/1917	04/12/1917
War Diary	Victory Camp Roclingcourt Sheet 51B. NW. G 3b	06/12/1917	31/12/1917
Heading	War Diary of D.A.D.V.S. 56th Division From January 1st 18 To January 31st 18 Vol 23		
War Diary	Victory Camp Roclingcourt Sheet 51B. NW G 3 b	01/01/1918	08/01/1918
War Diary	Mingoval Sheet 36b V 23b	09/01/1918	31/01/1918
War Diary	War Diary of D.A.D.V.S. 56th (London) Division From February 1918 To February 28th 1918 vol 24		
War Diary	Mingoval Sheet 36 B V 23.b	01/02/1918	08/02/1918
War Diary	Victory Camp Roclingcourt Sheet 51b NW G 3.b	11/02/1918	27/02/1918
Heading	War Diary of D.A.D.V.S. 56th (London) Division From 1-3-18 To 31-3-18 Vol 25		
War Diary	Victory Camp Roclingcourt Sheet 51b NW G 3.b.	01/03/1918	11/03/1918
War Diary	Anzin G 8 C 35 Sheet 51b NW	12/03/1918	26/03/1918

War Diary	Agnieres Sheet 51 C E2.c.1.1	27/03/1918	29/03/1918
Heading	War Diary of D.A.D.V.S. 56th (London) Division From April 1st 18 To April 30th 18 Vol 26		
War Diary	Agnieres E.2.C.1.1 Sheet 51C	01/04/1918	06/04/1918
War Diary	Berneville Q 6d 79 Sheet 51C	08/04/1918	08/04/1918
War Diary	Warlus K 36.6.5.7 Sheet 37 C	10/04/1918	30/04/1918
Heading	War Diary of D.A.D.V.S. 56th Division From 1-5-18 To 31-5-18 Vol 27		
War Diary	Warlus K 36.d.5.7 Sheet 57. C	01/05/1918	31/05/1918
Heading	War Diary of D.A.D.V.S. 56th Division From June 1st 18 To June 30th Vol 28		
War Diary	Warlus K 36.d.57 Sheet 51 C	01/06/1918	30/06/1918
War Diary		26/06/1918	30/06/1918
War Diary	War Diary Of D.A.D.V.S. 56th Division From July 1st 1918 To July 31-1918 Vol 29		
War Diary	Warlus K 37.d.57 Sheet 51 C	01/07/1918	14/07/1918
War Diary	Roellecourt T 20.d.55 Sheet 44 B	15/07/1918	17/07/1918
War Diary	Mingoval V 23 Central Sheet 44 B	18/07/1918	31/07/1918
Heading	War Diary of D.A.D.V.S. 56th Division From 1-8-18 To 31-8-18 Vol 30		
War Diary	Mingoval V 23 Central Sheet 44 B	01/08/1918	01/08/1918
War Diary	Warlus K 37.d.57 Sheet 51 C	02/08/1918	17/08/1918
War Diary	Le Cauroy N 6.a. 76 Sheet 51 C	18/08/1918	23/08/1918
War Diary	Basseux. X 3d 7.8-51 C	22/08/1918	29/08/1918
Heading	War Diary of D.A.D.V.S. 56th Division From September 1st 1918 To September 30-1918 Vol 31		
War Diary	Boileux S 11.a 5.8 (51b)	01/09/1918	06/09/1918
War Diary	Arras G 29.d 6.4. (51b)	08/09/1918	15/09/1918
War Diary	Les Fosses Farm N 12.a.53 (51b)	16/09/1918	27/09/1918
War Diary	Villers Cagnicourt P 32d C 51b	28/09/1918	30/09/1918
Heading	War Diary of D.A.D.V.S. 56th Division From 1-10-18 To 31-10-18 Vol 33		
War Diary	Villers Cagnicourt P 32.d. C Sh 51b	01/10/1918	15/10/1918
War Diary	Etrun L 3.d. Sht 51 C	16/10/1915	30/10/1915
War Diary	Bouchain	31/10/1918	31/10/1918
War Diary	Bassevilleh 35.d. 02	31/10/1918	31/10/1918
Heading	War Diary of D.A.D.V.S. 56th Division From November 1st 1918 To November 30/1918 Vol 34		
War Diary	Bouchain (Basseville) H 35.d. 02	01/11/1918	02/11/1918
War Diary	Saultain F 25.b.24	04/11/1918	07/11/1918
War Diary	Fayt Le Franc B 11.d.10.5 Sheet 51	09/11/1918	26/11/1918
War Diary	Harveing W 16.b. 2.4 Sheet 45	27/11/1918	29/11/1918
Heading	War Diary of D.A.D.V.S 56th Division.O/C 1/1st London M.V.S. From 1. Dec. 1918 To 31. Dec. 1918. Vol 35		
War Diary	Harveing W 16.b.2.4 Sht H5	01/12/1918	31/12/1918
Heading	War Diary of D.A.D.V.S 56th Division From January 1st To January 31st 1919 Vol 36		
War Diary	Harveing W 16.b.24 Sht 45	01/01/1919	31/01/1919
Heading	War Diary of D.A.D.V.S. 56th Division From February 1st 1919 To February 28-19 Vol 37		
War Diary	Harveing W 1.b. 2.4 Sht 45	02/02/1919	27/02/1919
Heading	1/1st London Mobile Veterinary Sector DADVS 56th Division War Diary March 1919 Vol 38		
War Diary	War Diary of D.A.D.V.S. 56th Division From March 1st 1919. To March 31st 1919		

War Diary	Harvengt W 166. 2.4 Sht 45	05/03/1919	24/03/1919
War Diary	Harvengt	25/03/1919	31/03/1919
War Diary	Jemappes (Belgium)	01/04/1919	30/04/1919

WO 95/29399/3

56TH DIVISION

ASST DIR. VETY SERVICES
MAR 1916 – APR 1919

Confidential

War Diary
of
A.D.V.S., 56th (London) Division

From March 1st 1916 To March 31st 1916

Vol II

ADVS 56 Div
Vol III

Army Form C. 2118

WAR DIARY
~~INTELLIGENCE SUMMARY~~
(Erase heading not required.)

Instructions regarding War Diaries and Intelligence Summaries are contained in F. S. Regs., Part II. and the Staff Manual respectively. Title pages will be prepared in manuscript.

Place	Date	Hour	Summary of Events and Information	Remarks and references to Appendices
DOMART	1.3.16		The Division was on this date practically complete with the exception of Divisional Cavalry & Mobile Vety. Section	
	2.3.16		The total number of horses in the Division is 4452. Horses sick for the week 143, Died 14, Evacuated 2. Evacuated to Lt. Col. 14. The chief ailments being of a prevalent kind nature.	
	12.3.16		Capt Domart proceeding by Road Route to DOULLENS.	
DOULLENS	12.3.16		Arrived Doullens.	
	9.3.16		Total horses 4438, Died 11, Evac. nil, Evacuated 9, Total Sick 195.	
	14.3.16		Mobile Vety. Sect. arrived for duty.	
	15.3.16		No 54/08,115 & Q.S. Titchener Pte A.S.C. arrived for duty as clerk in this Office	
	16.3.16		Lt-Doullens & arrived in 2nd Country. Total Horses 4407, Died 2, Sect 1, Evacuated 28, Total Sick 187.	
	23.3.16		Total Horses 4744, Died 8, Evac. 4, Evacuated 25, Total Sick 183. The horses belonging to the 3rd Divny. Dua. Coy A.V.C. were included in the charge.	
	30.3.16		Total horses 4997, Died 3, Evac. 3, Evacuated 31, Total Sick 208	
	31.3.16		The R.A.V.C. visited the R.D.C. Hospital the arrival of the Divist. Consider the large number of animals evacuated may be accounted for by the difficulty of horses cauth by the Remount Dept. Many are not fit for the work & have again to be evacuated.	

T.J.134. Wt. W708—776. 500000. 4/15. Sir J.C. & S.

T. Jeffords Major
A.D.V.S. 5th Div.

Army Form C. 2118.

WAR DIARY
INTELLIGENCE SUMMARY.
(Erase heading not required.)

Instructions regarding War Diaries and Intelligence Summaries are contained in F. S. Regs., Part II. and the Staff Manual respectively. Title pages will be prepared in manuscript.

Place	Date	Hour	Summary of Events and Information	Remarks and references to Appendices
LE CAUROY	1.4.16		Divisional H.Q. at LE CAUROY	
	2.4.16		Lt Collebrook to duty from leave	
	6.4.16		Total horses 4828, Brid H. Bat 1, Evacuated 6, Total Sick 166. Posted 19 Re Pick Bat 1, 4+2, 1 Res Regimental Dep	
	7.4.16		Captain Adams proceeded on leave	
	8.4.16		14.1 Remounts arrived in the Divn & were reported by me the strength of animals both H.Q. were of good quality & in good condition. The R animals altho' inherent condition satisfactorily in many cases	
	13.4.16		Total horses 5786, Brid 3 Strap 3, Evac 82, Total Sick 232. Thus little noticed of animals to units. Strays	
	15.4.16		Field 2/3, 3rd Res Bayt, Thug Battns 4/1, 2/3, 109 4/8, Coroll 67/1, 12, 2/3. Stragglers	
	17.4.16		Major Holmes returned from leave.	
	19.4.16		In order to maintain the strength of Smiths, an order was issued in D.R.O. that Units would send SE & I remen	
			to certain to qualified Farriers	
	20.4.16		Total horses 6268, Brid 5, Evac 19, Total Sick 27. Hd	
	21.4.16		116 = Army Trps, 11 Ro Cy R.E. attached for Rats purposes	
	25.4.16		2.8.15 one horse accidental two horse falling	
	26.4.16		24.T.S. went to 11th Dist Ree & Camp	
	27.4.16		Total horses 6282, Brid 5, Evac 3, Evac 21, Total Sick 233	
	30.4.16		Signed for duty from Rest Station	

J Sulliva Lt-Col
A.D.V.S. 56
1st Inf Div

WAR DIARY

INTELLIGENCE SUMMARY.

(Erase heading not required.)

Army Form C. 2118.

Instructions regarding War Diaries and Intelligence Summaries are contained in F. S. Regs., Part II. and the Staff Manual respectively. Title pages will be prepared in manuscript.

Place	Date	Hour	Summary of Events and Information	Remarks and references to Appendices
HENU	5.5.16		The Division moved to fresh Area with Head Quarters at Henu, leaving 3 Batty R.F.A. in the Area.	
MAP LENS 11			Total horses 5731, Died 7, Destroyed 1, Evacuated 32, Total Sick 190	
	7.5.16		N. 240 "O" Troop, 3rd Bridging Train R.E. attached to Division.	
	11.5.16		132 A.T. Coy. "C" Coy. 3rd Cop Battn. & 3rd Survey Coy attached to Division	
	12.5.16		Total horses 5664, Died 2, Destroyed 2, Evacuated 16, Total Sick 177	
	16.5.16		Left Half 3rd Bridging Train, & 114th H.B. R.G.A. were attached to the Division	
	19.5.16		Total horses 6044, Died 8, Destroyed 2, Evacuated 2, Total Sick 198	
	20.5.16		Report received that change was contemplated in 1/5 Brigades, upon visiting them I found all unnecessary for contents had been ordered by Capt Townsend & were carried out. Advised G.O.C. R.A. D.T.S.	
	22.5.16		27th Reserve Park attached to Division for Pty purposes. Saw G.O.C. respecting change.	
	24.5.16		131st H.B. R.G.A. attached to Division	
	26.5.16		Total horses 6088, Died 5, Destroyed 1, Evacuated 41, Total Sick 218.	
			During the month the D.A.C. of the Artillery Reserve attached to the D.A.C. This change caused a reduction in the number of horses. In the first half of the month 12 A.V.C. Sergts arrived for duty.	
	31.5.16		The Divisional Cavalry (one Sqdn 2nd K.E.H.) left the Division	

I. Gifford Capp.
A.D.V.S. 37th Division

ADVS 56 Army Form C. 2118.

FL 5

WAR DIARY
INTELLIGENCE SUMMARY.
(Erase heading not required.)

Place	Date	Hour	Summary of Events and Information	Remarks and references to Appendices
HENU	2.6.16		Captain Colt met with an accident by being dragged by horse.	
	2.6.16		Total horses 5567, Died 4, Evacuated 2, Sick 23, missing 3, Total Sick 211	
	3.6.16		Captain Colt evacuated to Hospital	
	4.6.16		114th Heavy Battery R.G.A. left the Division & was replaced by the 135th H.B. R.G.A.	
	5.6.16		Advice received that Lieut. J.R. Staples A.V.C. (T.C.) should join for duty in lieu of Capt. Colt.	
	7.6.16		The Army Commander paid a visit to the "Bridoon" Sh. V. Sect.	
	9.6.16		Total horses 5524, Died 2, Sick 4, Evacuated 33, Total Sick 201	
	10.6.16		The D.D.V.S. paid visit of inspection to H.V.S. He Divisional Commander also inspected the horses.	
	11.6.16		Lieut. Staples A.V.C. reported for duty.	
	16.6.16 22.6.16 23.6.16		Total horses 5515, Sick 1, Died 1, Evacuated 7 Total 170. 31 heart amongst animals by friendly fire. Total horses 5628, Died 5, Sick 1, Evacuated 15, Total Sick 207	
	27.6.16		Established an Advanced Collecting Station: Knell (circular Road) for Mature animals HENU Hospital about 6' 2' about it. Also reported to D.V.S. state of horses Battery 281st Bde R.F.A.	
*	30.6.16		D.D.V.S. inspected 261st Bde. R.F.A. during the week, 1 horse killed by gun shot, 4B wounded Total horses 5404, Died 5, Sick 1, Evac #5, missing 1, Total Sick 257.	
*	28.6.16		Capt Bonnerud was sent to 3.A. sick	

J. Hibbard Lieut
ADVS 56th Division

ADVS 56
Mob Vety Sec
Vol 5

WAR DIARY

INTELLIGENCE SUMMARY
(Erase heading not required.)

Army Form C. 2118.

Place	Date	Hour	Summary of Events and Information	Remarks and references to Appendices
HENU	1.7.16			
	2.7.16		Captain Townsend returned to duty from Rest Station	
	4.7.16		Mobile Vety Section removed from HURTEBISE FARM to D13, L9 & Ref. Sheet 57d.	
	6.7.16		No of animals 5369, Evac 41, Died 9, Dest 4, Sick 262. 13 Wounds of which 7 Died.	
	11.7.16		Mobile Vety. Sect. removed from D13, L-9.4 to HURTEBISE FARM	
	12.7.16		Collected surplus Equipment from 27th Reserve Park & handed it to M.V.S. for transfer to Base	
	13.7.16		Inspected Brit. Train transported outbreak of mange	
	13.7.16		Animals 5328, Evac 36, Died 2, Dest 2, Sick 225. One Enrolment returned	
	15.7.16		Took over Army Corps Troops attd. to 37th Div at request of A.D.V.S. as his Div. was moving	
	15.7.16		Lt. Heavey's Agreement arrived for signature.	
	16.7.16		Mobile Vety. Sect. removed to GRINCOURT. a/c.	
	17.7.16		Ssgt Smitherman sent to HAVRE from 28th Dec R.F.A. replaced by Sergt. Meacham R.F.A.	
	19.7.16		Asked by Q for report as to quality of Oats. Replied	
	20.7.16		Animals 5900, Evac 58, Died 1, Dest 3 Sick 231. 3 Wounds 1 of which died	
	22.7.16		Lieut Somerville reported his arrival for duty ex 90 to VIII Corps	
	24.7.16		Remounts arrived 90 of which were not issued owing to suspected Mange & two Lame.	
	24.7.16		Lieut Heavey's agreement returned duly signed & witnessed	

Army Form C. 2118.

WAR DIARY
or
INTELLIGENCE SUMMARY.
(Erase heading not required.)

Instructions regarding War Diaries and Intelligence Summaries are contained in F. S. Regs., Part II. and the Staff Manual respectively. Title pages will be prepared in manuscript.

Place	Date	Hour	Summary of Events and Information	Remarks and references to Appendices
HENU	27/7		Arrivals 5 3 34, Evac 31 Died 1, Sick 1, Sick 189 - 1 Gun shot which died	
	29/7		Received visit from D.D.V.S.	
	30/7		Reported outbreak of Mange in 283rd Bde. R.F.A.	
	31/7		Further report as to 285th Bde R.F.A. During the month there were 57 cases of Mange or suspected Mange evacuated from the Division. There were no other Contagious diseases.	

Richard Hughes
1. Richard Hughes
A.D.V.S. 52 Division

WAR DIARY
INTELLIGENCE SUMMARY
(Erase heading not required.)

Army Form C. 2118.

ADVS Vol 6

Place	Date	Hour	Summary of Events and Information	Remarks and references to Appendices
HENU	1.8.16		Visited R.F.A. Wagon Lines	
	3.8.16		Visited Bayencourt & reported S.H.2. as to horse standings	
	5.8.16		Strength of Animals 5370, Evac 35, Died 2, Dest 1. Total sick 193	
	6.8.16		Inspected Rubires ri MANGE R.F.A.	
	7.8.16		Inspected 262nd Brigade ground & cases Trup Mange R.F.A.	
			Others 2 382nd " " 2 more cases Trup Mange. Although cases in "B" & "C" Batteries 4"D" Battery had many him horses.	
	8.8.16		" 169th Inf Bde also 2/2 & 2/1 Field Amb. 78 Remounts arrived 2 cases of Surat Mange amongst them.	
	10.8.16		Strength 5401, Evac 52, Died 1, Dest 1. Total Sick 179	
	11.8.16		Inspected 1 Bty. 287 - Bde R.F.A.	
	12.8.16		" 3 " " 281 " "	
			" " N.2. & B. Troops Purston Park	
	15.8.16		" 168th Infantry Bde & 2/2 Field Cy R.E.	
	16.8.16		Received visit from A.D.V.S. 17th Division	
	17.8.16		Strength 5379, Evac 21, Died 3, Dest 1. Total Sick 145 — × 1 killed by gunshot	
	20.8.16		A.D.V.S Third Army & A.D.V.S. 17th Div. visited me. Performed P.M. on Flanders & Morris 147	

Army Form C. 2118

WAR DIARY
INTELLIGENCE SUMMARY
(Erase heading not required.)

Instructions regarding War Diaries and Intelligence Summaries are contained in F. S. Regs., Part II. and the Staff Manual respectively. Title pages will be prepared in manuscript.

Place	Date	Hour	Summary of Events and Information	Remarks and references to Appendices
HENU	20.8.16		Reported to D.D.V.S. no traces of Glanders at MONDICOURT.	
DOULLENS	21.8.16		H.Q. of Division marched to DOULLENS – M.V.S. to MILLY	
FROHEN LE GRAND	22.8.16		H.Q. of Division marched to FROHEN LE GRAND – M.V.S. to OUTREBOIS	
ST RIQUIER	23.8.16		H.Q. of Division marched to ST. RIQUIER – M.V.S. to CAOURS	
	24.8.16		Strength 5357, Evac 19, Died 5, Destr 1 — + 2 Gunshot wounds x + 2 Gunshot wounds	
	27.8.16		Advised by D.D.V.S. one horse N.I.H. evacuated by our M.V.S. reacted to Mallein – gave tested Glanders wounded	
	28.8.16		All horses in M.V.S. mallined –	
	29.8.16		No reactions in horses of M.V.S.	
	30.8.16		Went to Abbeville to put out Mallein to test whole of horses in 282nd Bde. R.F.A. whose horses had rested at Troughs as N.I.H. – Instructed V.O. i/c to test all horses in 282nd Bde. R.F.A.	
	31.8.16		Strength 5374, Evac 10, Died 3, Destr 1 + — +Glanders	

A. Millar Major
1. D.V.S. 56
O.V.S.

Vol 7

Confidential
War Diary
of
56th (London) Division
A.D.V.S.
From September 1st 1916.
To. September 30th 1916

Original

WAR DIARY or INTELLIGENCE SUMMARY.

Army Form C. 2118

(Erase heading not required.)

Place	Date	Hour	Summary of Events and Information	Remarks and references to Appendices
ST RIQUIER	1-9-16	—	Issued orders to 1st Ld. M.V.S. to move to LONGPRE with Headquarter Transport entrained.	
"	3-9-16	—	M.V.S. and Headquarters (Div) Transport move to LONGPRE by road.	
"	4-9-16	—	Headquarter unit moves to CORBIE by rail. M.V.S. moved to DAOURS from LONGPRE.	
CORBIE	5-9-16	—	Headquarters at CORBIE. M.V.S. at DAOURS.	
"	6-9-16	—	Headquarter unit moved to "FORKED TREE" camp. Ref: L.26.1.1. Reference Sheet 62D.	
			M.V.S. moved to camp L.6.d.3.5. Map sheet 62D.	
L.26.1.1. Sheet 62D	7-9-16	—	Administrative Headquarters moved to "CITADEL" camp F.21.c. Sheet 62D. Advanced Headquarters established at "BILLON FARM" F.24.c central Sheet 62D. M.V.S. moved to F.26.a.2.6. Sheet 62D.	
F.21.c. Sheet 62D	7-9-16	—	Strength 4,916, Evac: 25, Died 2, Seat 1, Total Sick 128. × 1 Killed Lunahan W.S.	
"	8-9-16	—	24th Div Artillery and three V.O.s came under my administration.	
"	11-9-16	—	Situated at BOIS DE TAILLES Sheet 62D.	
"			16th Div Artillery with 3096 animals and three V.O.s came under my administration.	
"			Situated at "CARNOY" Sheet 62D. 24th D.A. moved to MINDEN POST near CARNOY. Sheet 62D.	
"	12-9-16	—	Visited 24 Div Artillery H.Q. regarding supply of water for their animals. Following casualties in 16 Division Artillery due to hostile fire. A/177 Bdr R.F.A. 12 killed, D/177 Bde R.F.A. 4 killed, D/177 Bde R.Q. four killed.	

W.H. Anckorn Capt. A.V.C. (T)
A/A.D.V.S. 16 Division

WAR DIARY
or
INTELLIGENCE SUMMARY.
(Erase heading not required.)

Army Form C. 2118

Place	Date	Hour	Summary of Events and Information	Remarks and references to Appendices
F21+55 Sheet 62D	14.9.16	–	Administrative H.Q. moved to BILLON FARM F24c central Sheet 62D. Advd. H.Q. moves further forward. Total Strength 10446. Evac: 71. Died 24. Destroyed 21. Total Sick 365. (Killed by Shell fire 24). Destroyed after wounds 15."	
F24 central Sheet 62D	15/9/16	–	Y.O's meeting.	
"	16-9-16	–	Visited all Infantry Bns with D.A.+Q.M.G.	
"	17-9-16	–	Visited 46th Mobile Vety Section MEAULTE to meet S.D.V.S. Fourth Army. Discussed Casualty Clearing Station to be established at MEAULTE under Capt PHIPPS A.V.C.	
"	20/9/16	–	MAJOR T. HIBBARD, A.V.C. A.D.V.S. 56 Division evacuated to Hospital with affection of the eye. Administrative HQ moved back to F21 c 56. Sheet 62D	
F21+56 Sheet 62D	21/9/16	–	Y.O's meeting. Capt. H.L. ANTHONY, A.V.C. T.F. appointed Acting A.D.V.S.	
"	23-9-16	–	Y.6.th. 282nd Bde R.F.A. reports eight deaths due to Shell fire in his Brigade. Total Strength 10989. Evac: 75. Died 16. Dest 10. Total Sick 365 (19 deaths due to Shell fire)	
"	26-9-16	–	Advice received of CAPT E.T. TOMLIN A.N.C. joining Division for temporary duty from No.4 Vet. Hosp.	
"	28/9/16	–	Y6+16b Bde R.F.A reported following casualties in that Bde due to hostile air raid. 6 animals killed, 20 destroyed after wounds. CAPT TOMLIN A.V.C. reported for duty & was	
"	29-9-16	–	posted to 282nd Bde R.F.A. temporarily. Total Strength 10801. Evac: 106. Died 28. Dest 32. Total Sick 444 (4 deaths due to Shell fire). W.A. Auchery Capt. A.V.C. (T) a/A.D.V.S. 56 Division	

Original

Vol 5

Confidential
War Diary
of
A.D.V.S. 56th (London) Division

From October 1st 1916 to October 31st 1916

WAR DIARY
INTELLIGENCE SUMMARY.

(Erase heading not required.)

Army Form C. 2118.

Instructions regarding War Diaries and Intelligence Summaries are contained in F. S. Regs., Part II. and the Staff Manual respectively. Title pages will be prepared in manuscript.

Place	Date	Hour	Summary of Events and Information	Remarks and references to Appendices
F21 & 55 Sheet 62D	1/10/16	—	Administrative Divl H.Q. moved to MUD POINT A8.c.0.3. Sheet 62C	
Ascos Sheet 62C	2/10/16	—	Artillery Wagon lines moved up to POMMIERS REDOUBT. A1.5. Sheet 62C	
"	4/10/16	—	Casualties (3 Lmen killed outright and 3 destroyed after wounds) occurred. 1st Edmbro Field Coy R.E. and 6 Lmes killed outright of 282nd Brigade R.F.A. all by Shell fire.	
"	6/10/16	—	D.D.V.S. Fourth Army visited 1st Lon Mobile Veterinary Section and saw Capt ANTHONY Acting A.D.V.S. Total Strength 492 H. Evacuated 42. Died 25. Destroyed 11. Total Lost 260 (26 Deaths due to Shell fire). During week 16th and 24th Divl Artillery left this area.	
"	7/10/16	—	56 Division "Q" advised Successor to MAJOR HIBBARD A.V.C (T.F.) to be CAPT ASCOTT A.V.C (T.F.)	
"	10/10/16	—	Administrative D.H.Q. returned to "THE CITADEL" F21 & 55. Sheet 62D. Advanced H.Q. also moved to same place. 56 Division less Artillery and No 169 Inf Train prepare to move out of action. Rec. Detached Capt BERRY A.V.C. from 282nd Brigade R.F.A. & attached him to 169 Infantry Bde.	
F21 & 55 Sheet 62D	11/10/16	—	Divl H.Q. moved to BELLOY SUR SOMME. D.H.Q. Transport and M.V.S. move by road to DAOURS. All Division less Artillery move & take up new area around BELLOY.	L. L. Little Lt. Col A.V.C A.D.V.S. 56 Division
BELLOY SUR SOMME	12/10/16	—	D.H.Q. Transport and M.V.S. arrive at BELLOY SUR SOMME	

Army Form C. 2118.

WAR DIARY
or
INTELLIGENCE SUMMARY.
(Erase heading not required.)

Place	Date	Hour	Summary of Events and Information	Remarks and references to Appendices
BELLOY SUR SOMME	13.10.16	—	Total Strength (less Artillery) 1422. Evacuated 11? Died 6 Destroyed 3 Total Sick 194 (5 Deaths from Gunshot Wounds)	
"	14.10.16	—	CAPT W. ASCOTT A.V.C (T.F.) arrived to take over A.D.V.S. from 123 Division	
"	16.10.16	—	Issued orders to CAPT E.J. TOMLIN A.V.C. (T.C.), who was attached to this Division for temporary duty, to proceed to 12th Division reporting on arrival to A.D.V.S.	
"	17.10.16	—	CAPT E.J. TOMLIN A.V.C. proceeded to join 12th Division. A.D.V.S. attended conference at office of D.D.V.S. Main Theme on leaving M.V.S. with Artillery on the line when Infantry move out	
"	18.10.16	—	Orders received for move of Division to HALLENCOURT area on 20th inst	
HALLENCOURT	20.10.16	—	Divl H.Q. and M.V.S. move to HALLENCOURT. Total Strength 1784 Evacuated 20 Sick Nil Destroyed 2 Total Sick 48.	
"	23.10.16	—	Division moves by rail to First Army Area to take over from 61st Division. D.H.Q. moves to LESTREM Sheet 36A. M.V.S. moves to CORNET MALO Reference K32c Sheet 36A	
"	24.10.16	—	A.D.V.S. visited A.D.V.S. 61st Division with a view to taking over in a day or two.	
LESTREM	25.10.16	—	D.D.V.S. First Army visited A.D.V.S. today & gave instructions re returns etc.	
"	26.10.16	—	Total Strength 1825 Evacuated 1 Died 4 Destroyed 1 Total Sick 66	
"	27.10.16	—	[signature] Capt A.V.C. A.D.V.S. 56 Division	

T.131. Wt. W708—776. 500000. 4/15. Sir J. C. & 9.

Army Form C. 2118.

WAR DIARY
or
INTELLIGENCE SUMMARY.
(Erase heading not required.)

Instructions regarding War Diaries and Intelligence Summaries are contained in F.S. Regs., Part II. and the Staff Manual respectively. Title pages will be prepared in manuscript.

Place	Date	Hour	Summary of Events and Information	Remarks and references to Appendices
LESTREM Sheet 36A	28-10-16	—	D.H.Q moved to LA GORGUE Sheet 36A. M.V.S moved and took over old billets of 61st Divisional M.V.S at LA GORGUE L.25 d.5.5. Sheet 36A.	
LA GORGUE Sheet 36A	30-10-16	—	The 500th (How) Battery R.F.A. arrived from England for attachment to this Division, with 160 horses	
—	31-10-16	—	A.D.V.S visited 500th (How) Battery R.F.A. situated at R.3 c.5.3. Sheet 36A. Half of the animals are in fair condition, the other half poor. From this area evacuations take place by barge to ST OMER. First evacuation thus was made by my M.V.S this day, 31-10-16. CAPT E BERRY A.V.C proceeded on short leave to England this date	

W. J. Kenn Capt A.V.C
A.D.V.S 56 Division

ADVS 55 / JHG

Army Form C. 2118

WAR DIARY
INTELLIGENCE SUMMARY
(Erase heading not required.)

Instructions regarding War Diaries and Intelligence Summaries are contained in F.S. Regs., Part II. and the Staff Manual respectively. Title pages will be prepared in manuscript.

Place	Date	Hour	Summary of Events and Information	Remarks and references to Appendices
LA GORGUE	1-11-16	-	Visited My Sec. 61st D.A.C. out with 9r Dunn QVC. and found suspicious cases of Skin Disease.	
134 Staf				
36 A	3-11-16	-	Reported to A.D.V.S. First Army on 500 (How) By R.A. which joined the Division on 30-10-16.	
	4-11-16		Inspected the three Field Ambulances with A.D.M.S. Found rather poor animals two of them. Total Strength 502Y Evacuated 16. Died 4 Destroyed 2. Total Sick 165.	
	5-11-16		Attended office of A.D.V.S. First Army WH conference.	
	6-11-16		Arranged with M. JULES DELOS of ESTAIRES to take all horses + mules fit for consumption at an all round price of 105 francs.	
	9-11-16		Visited My Sec. 61st D.A.C. + sent 8 more suspected cases of Mange to M.V.S.	
	10-11-16		A.D.V.S. proceeded on short leave to England today. Total Stgth 5214 Evac 29 Died 4 Dest 4 Total Sick 215.	
	12-11-16		A.D.V.S. First Army visited 74 Sec. 61st D.A.C. re Mange.	
	16-11-16		A.D.V.S. First Army inspected 61st Divl Artillery today with O.R.A. Sent quite a number of animals to M.V.S. Total Stgth 5230 Evac 39 Died 3 Dest 3 Total Sick 235.	
	18-11-16 to 20-11-16		61st Divl Artillery MYSY 61st Divl Train, mine out of this area and are replaced by 6th Divl Artilley + MY by 6th Divl Train. A.D.V.S. returned from France.	

Wm Jamul McAir
ADVS 45th Division

WAR DIARY
or
INTELLIGENCE SUMMARY.
(Erase heading not required.)

Army Form C. 2118

Instructions regarding War Diaries and Intelligence Summaries are contained in F. S. Regs., Part II. and the Staff Manual respectively. Title pages will be prepared in manuscript.

Place	Date	Hour	Summary of Events and Information	Remarks and references to Appendices
LAGORGUE SH: 36A	22.11.16		Visited 167-168 Infantry Bdes with Capt Berry ATC.	
			Capt Anthony O/C 1/1 London M.T.S. taken to 2/1 London F.A. suffering from P.U.O.	
	23 "		Visited Mobile Vet. Section. Rumours of Station. Capt. Hutch my taken to Corps Officers Rest Station at Merville. (Total Meningite? +891. Evacuated 109 Sick & Amb.)	
	"		Morning 11 T.O's at my office.	
	24 "		Total Sick 456.	
	28 "		Inspected 2/1 London F.C. R.E. Inspected 1/4 (QWR) + Mov Section to DAC	
	30 "		Visited & inspected 38 Brigade R.F.A. (Total Meningite 4880 Evacuated 159 Sick.& Destroyed 3 Total Sick 369.)	

A.J.R. Wright LtC
A.D.M.S. 56" Division

Vol 10

Confidential
War Diary
of
A.D.V.S. 56th (Lond) Division

From December 1st 1916
To December 31st 1916

WAR DIARY
or
INTELLIGENCE SUMMARY.

(Erase heading not required.)

Army Form C. 2118.

Place	Date	Hour	Summary of Events and Information.	Remarks and references to Appendices
LA GORGUE L34 Sheet 36A	1-12-16		Capt. Anthony returned to duty at H/London Mob: Vet. Sect. Inspected 1/3 London Horse Ambce. Stables much improved. V.O.'s meeting at my office.	
	2-12-16		Inspected horses of 1/68 Inf/Bde with C.O. + Army. Lieut Staples 1NCO + 5 men with a Revt. went to Arnhell (from the H/London Mob: Sect) to meet the 56th Artillery + render assistance if required.	
	3-12-16		Lieut Staples + party returned from Arnhell.	
	5-12-16		Capt. J. Morcard reported arrival at 4 Capt. Jordans reported arrival at 4 Remount.	
	6-12-16		Attended conference of ADSC's at DDVS's office at Sillery. Capt. Adams wind-on admitted to England, Capt. J Morcard reported arrival at Remount.	
	7-12-16		Inspected Army Troops Transport 1st Div. Pontoon Park. 265th Co RE + 257 Co RE.	
	8 . .		V.O's meeting at my office. Capt. Anthony left at 10·45 p.m. for short leave to England.	
	9 . .		Inspected 1/5 Cheshire Bait'llion + found 2 more cases of mange. Total strength 5122	
			Evacuated 19. Died 4. Destroyed 4. Total sick 154.	
	10 . .		Inspected H.Q. D.A.C. 61st Div: horses + found 23 cases of mange which on microscopical examination found to be sarcoptic. These were sent to 1/1 Mrs + evacuated between 10th + 11th.	
	12 . .		Inspected 1/1 B.A.C. again Found 3 more cases of mange.	
	14 . .		Total strength 5119. Evacuated 59. Died 4. Destroyed 2. Total sick 186.	
	15 . .		V.O's meeting at my office. Arranged for lectures + demonstrations to Young Officers + NCO's	
	18 . .		Capt. Adams ret. from leave. Inspected 251st Bde RFA with Capt Heaney.	

W. J. Newman Major ?
ADVS 2nd Div
2-1-17

WAR DIARY
or
INTELLIGENCE SUMMARY.
(Erase heading not required.)

Army Form C. 2118

Place	Date	Hour	Summary of Events and Information	Remarks and references to Appendices
[France]	19.12.16		Inspected H.Q. 4 No 3 Section D.A.C.	
	21...		Inspected 281st Brigade with Capt. Townsend. 2nd Inspected 280th Brigade with Capt. Freeman. Total strength 5729. Evacuated 33 Sick 8 (2 by impaction) Destroyed 2. Total sick 167.	
	...		Inspected horse & 6 Reserve Parks at Inglem & Sadt. & Anne: Trench at Bapel Farm.	
	26		D.A.F.O. visited. Inspected A.S.C. horses & H.Q. & 2 & 3 sections & D.A.C. Shrunken arms & appearance of bad shoes, ammunition which had been issued. Hind shoes had sharper badly held-for calks & so weakened by the last that they were continually breaking. Have suggested that — it would greatly improve the appearance notified — if the saddles in future were issued 1" deep until the future amount. This would be more economical & save the times & expense now caused by having to return the watch maft. when new saddles are required. Capt Harvey evacuated today for scabies. Visited ADVS 37th Div: & attaching intervention by Army from M.V.Ss. 28th Inspected 167th Infantry horses with Rig Gen Field.	
	29 ...		Inspected horses prepared for casting & other detachments with D.D. Remounts. Total strength 5702. Evacuated 24 Sick 2. Destroyed 1. Total sick 140.	
	31...		General remarks. Shipping not nearly complete. Employing to the inadequate supply & harnesses. The only units at all fourth furnished their own machines. Major Maj: ARC TF ADVS 56th Div: 2-1-17	

Vol XI

Confidential

War Diary
of
A.D.M.S. 56th London Division

From January 1st 1919

c.o. Fenway Blovey?

WAR DIARY
or
INTELLIGENCE SUMMARY.
(Erase heading not required.)

Army Form C. 2

Place	Date	Hour	Summary of Events and Information	Remarks and references to Appendices
LAGORGUE	1.1.17		Inspected 2/1 & 2/3 Field Ambulance. Found horses much improved. 2nd Inspected No 4 Co Div. Train with Lt. Col. Galloway & Capt Anthony & found 1 Case of Mange, inspected 10 including 3 found by me in this Unit yesterday.	
L34	2.1.17		3/– 52 Remounts arrived for the Division. 40 they were inspected by Capt Anthony for the D.A.C. lines. They were not inspected on arrival at Rail Head as I received no	
Hut 36 A	3.1.17		5/– Notice of their arrival. 5/– total strength 6705. Evacuated 45 Died 4 Destroyed 2 Total strength 190	
	3.1.17		Meeting H.Q. at army office. Inspected B3/282. Many very thin horses. Query ? to ability +	
	5.1.17		found 5 cases of subject Mange. Clipping very backward.	
	6 " "		Insp No I ASC Found 3 cases of Mange. Insp– H.Q.Div: Horse Camp Mange – Rain heavy.	
	" "		Insp: E/252 & train horses inspected mauls to H.Q. Horses & R.A. Card. 10 for stability–	
	8 " "		Reported to AVts Masters re am. Hospitals & Hospitals. Suggested more horses being required	
	10 " "		by Ordnance for purchase. Shortening in majority of cases and there is now little... [illegible]	
	" "		Inspected 58 Remounts. Capt Kenny proceeds on short leave to Ireland. Meeting of H.Q.s	
	12 " "		at army office. Intel Strength 5039 Evacuated 29 Died 6 Destroyed 1. Total sick 145.	
	" "		Attended conference of A.Ds.V.S. at Chocques. 15th inspected 2– + 3– sections of R.A.C. Conditions of	
	14 " "		2nd very bad indeed lines being unsatisfactory. Reported to Q + A.D.V.S. trans giving this fact.	
	16 " "		Inspected 24 Remounts at the station LaGorgue. 19 Meeting H.Q.s at army office. Lt. Shaw. Maj. Huff.	
	18 " "			ADVS 1st Division

Army Form C. 2118

WAR DIARY
or
INTELLIGENCE SUMMARY.
(Erase heading not required.)

Instructions regarding War Diaries and Intelligence Summaries are contained in F. S. Regs., Part II. and the Staff Manual respectively. Title pages will be prepared in manuscript.

Place	Date	Hour	Summary of Events and Information	Remarks and references to Appendices
LA GORGUE L34 Sheet 36A	19.1.17		Total Strength 5022. Evacuated 39. Sick 2. Destroyed 1. Total Sick 145. 20th Entertainment	
	20.1.17		Returned to duty from sick leave. 21st Inspected No 1 Sec. D.A.C. & Transport convoy of Manager.	
	22.		Capt Heany returned from leave. Capt Townsend proceeded on leave to England.	
	23rd & 24th		Inspected all Veterinary Parades & found many deficiencies which referred to A.D.V.S. Inspected reinforcements Brennan & train with Colonel Galloway at Reserve Mehuille. Purgavel. Attended conference at Q office re Corps Scheme. 26th D.D.V.S. visited & inspected all the Horses	
	26th		of the Artillery & D.A.C. in the Division. His report on the whole good.	
	"		Total Strength 5051. Evacuated 46. Died 1. Destroyed 5. Total Sick 142.	
	29th & 31st		Made a careful inspection of 165th 168th & 169th Brigades R.E. Companies. With the exception	
	30th		of the 6th Middleton which have quite had a good deal of the 513 (Indian) Co. which have many thin	
	31st		horses still. (Notation regarding those) of the Indians Regt where horses shew a distinct improvement from still how, the whole of the horses are much improved in a satisfactory condition.	

Lieut. Major. A.T. TF
A.D.V.S. 57th Division

Vol 2

Confidential
War Diary
of
A.D.V.S, 56th (Lodan Division)

From February 1-1917
To February 28-1917

Army Form C. 2118.

WAR DIARY
or
INTELLIGENCE SUMMARY.
(Erase heading not required.)

Instructions regarding War Diaries and Intelligence Summaries are contained in F. S. Regs., Part II. and the Staff Manual respectively. Title pages will be prepared in manuscript.

Place	Date	Hour	Summary of Events and Information	Remarks and references to Appendices
LA GORGUE	2.3.14		Total strength 5045. Evacuated 14 Died 1 Destroyed 3 Total sick 125	
March 36A	" "		Meeting of Veterinary Officers in my office. 4th Conference of ADVS at DDVS Office Bailleul	
	5 "		Inspected 4B No 1 horse at Essart. Signals 11th RA. All in fair condition improved	
	6 "		Visit Berlin with O/C 11th London MVS to see sheep hurdles constructed in the Canadian Division for sheeping horses affected with lice or skin disease.	
	7 "		Inspected 252 R.F.A. Royal Artillery Col. 1 sick, all improvement except in 252 B which has a great number of hover thin horses & Mules 4/10 NO [illegible]	
	8 "		Hour for lengthy visit. In 1st Army T.D. supply depot Salaud. Cap.[?] Lawrence followed by lunch. Total Strength 5144 evacuated — Died 2 Destroyed 6 Total sick 115	
	9 "		Inspected 12 Remount of B[?] & C Lines M263 Army T.D. all in hard condition. Captain Cochran on the 6th. No Mule has been given one in three. Mules first & to be supplied on the 6th — Died — Destroyed — leaving Capt Anthony	
	10 "		O/C 11th London M.V.S. on my deputy. 109 Remount arrived to the 5th Division to the 252 Bty Army F.A. Several men suffering from debility & unfit to serve. The ADVS 2nd Army visited & examined horses in the 13th & rejected 10. TJ total strength 6331 Evacuated 12 Died 1 Destroyed 4 Total sick 180. In the 1st Division of the D/E Manger room on the DVC	

[Signature] Major A/C ADVS [illegible]

WAR DIARY
or
INTELLIGENCE SUMMARY.
(Erase heading not required.)

Army Form C. 2118.

Place	Date	Hour	Summary of Events and Information	Remarks and references to Appendices
LA GORGUE L 34 Sht 36 A	16.1.17		found to have reappeared. Owing to lack of men the clipping of this section was very backward & the horses very dirty & to this the outbreak must be attributed. During the extremely cold weather the ponies in no dormant state but with its stress became active again. During the cold weather 6 horses in the same section but field rapidly & few had to be destroyed.	
	" " "		P.M. Evans's revealed myriads of strongylogenesis & tetracanthus. The litter & men were examined.	
	22. " "		Returned from leave. Return for week ending 20 Total Strength 5720 evacuated 79	
	" " "		Died 3 Battery discharged to Head sick 186. The large number of evacuations was due to many	
	" " "		the debility retakes mostly from the 282 Army FA Bde of cases which had been tried & of importance to buy period but which the cold wet about the influence cold weather.	
	24. " "		24 Reinforcement arrived for the 65 Nov: 4 & for the 282 Army F.A. Bde. Inspected No 2 dist:	
	26		N.M.F.C. 26" Inspected 6 Churches & 3/1 & 2/2 field Ambulance transfer horses	

[signature] Lieut Major ADVS 61 Div:

Vol 13

Original

Confidential

War Diary

of

56th U.S. 56th (London) Division

From March 1st 1917
To March 31st 1917

Army Form C. 2118.

WAR DIARY
or
INTELLIGENCE SUMMARY.
(Erase heading not required.)

Instructions regarding War Diaries and Intelligence Summaries are contained in F. S. Regs., Part II. and the Staff Manual respectively. Title pages will be prepared in manuscript.

Place	Date	Hour	Summary of Events and Information	Remarks and references to Appendices
LA GORGUE L34	1-3-17		Inspected 2SoD & 2/2 Field Ambulance Transport. 2nd V.O's meeting at my Office.	
Lhuisea	2-3-17		Inspected horses unconnected carefully for Strangles contagion.	
	3-3-17		Inspected 261 "Bde & 262" Army F.A. Bde. 1st Annual Meeting of A.D's S at A.D.M.S Office LILLERS	
WAIL LENS II	5.6.7.14		Divisions command unknown. 6.3.17. Marched to WAIL. 8th Marched to Cavany LE CAUROY	
LE CAUROY	10.3.17		M.V.S. arrived at LE CAUROY. 10th Inspected 169 at GODY en ARTOIS. 12th Inspected 169th	
	12.3.17		168th Brigades at BEAUDRICOURT IVERGNY & SUS ST LEGER. Visiting Very hard at BEAUDRICOURT	
	13.3.17		168 M.G.C. Very unsatisfactory. 13th Inspected 613 R.E.F.C. Improved but still unsatisfactory	
	16.3.17		V.O's meeting in my Office. 17th Inspected 1/6 Cheshires at WANQUETIN 250 + 251 R.F.A Rdes at	
	17.3.17		SIMENCOURT Both D Batteries unsatisfactory also 1/4 Middlesex in same village.	
	14.3.17		Inspected DAC at BAYINCOURT & 1/4 Cav Div. Train except B Echelon M.T.C. all unsatisfactory	
			2/3 London F.A. Ambulatory. 14th H.Q. moved to BEAUMETZ LES LOGES but may other Units Y Was	
	17.3.17		MVS remains at LE CAUROY. Inspected B.C. Division at BEAUDRICOURT. Horses been but	
	19.3.17		in hard condition. Nothing very bad. 21st Visited H.Q at BEAUMETZ Inspected 1/6 Cheshires at WANQUETIN	
	19.3.17		this unit has had a trying time since leaving LAVENTIE when they had ricollem comeed standing	
	21-3-17		Ponies still under suspicion for Mange this man had to be withdrawn but all things considered	
	21.3.17		they are standing well. 22nd Inspected 1/6 H.C at the IVERGNY & MG at OPPY. Both unsatisfactory.	

MStewartMajor
ADVS 56 Div.

2353 Wt W2541/1454 700,000 5/15 D. D. & L. A.D.S.S./Forms/C. 2118.

Army Form C. 2118.

WAR DIARY
or
INTELLIGENCE SUMMARY.
(Erase heading not required.)

Instructions regarding War Diaries and Intelligence
Summaries are contained in F. S. Regs., Part II.
and the Staff Manual respectively. Title pages
will be prepared in manuscript.

Place	Date	Hour	Summary of Events and Information	Remarks and references to Appendices
BEAUMETZ LÈS LOGES Sheet 51c Q 23	23.3.17		Moved to BEAUMETZ-LES-LOGES.	
	26.3.17		Mobile Veterinary Section moved to BEAUMETZ-LES-LOGES. 24th Visited 293rd Bde AFA at WAILLY 25th Inspected A/161 Q horses.	
	27.3.17		Inspected 280th & 281st Bde RFA.	
	28.3.17		Brigade ammunition columns & 7th Middlesex. 1st Middlesex 512 & 513 F.Co's RE & 167th Brigade. D Battery in bvt 28th Inspected 16th div NAC & ASC Corps & 416 Bt Co RE's	
	29.3.17		Inspected 293rd AFA. B.A.C. Manufacturing. Inspected 293 Bde A.F.A. D Batt vy I hrs & had	
	30.3.17		made no report on inspection of Division. 165 Bde 11th (Ser) Middlesex) & 3 Field Ambulances complety inspection of Division	
	31.3.17		Summary. A great number of the horses animals have suffered from exposure (even leaving LA GORGUE) Ablutions forward the line having appreciated by a shortage of animals particularly in the Artillery D.A.C & A.S.C. Owing to the clipping not having been completed until recently the short coats were appreciated with the resulting starting there has been an alarming increase in debility & death & destruction.	

Major,
Staff 56 Division

31-3-17

Vol 14

Confidential
War Diary
of
A.D.V.S. 56th Division
From April 1st 1917
To April 30th 1917

WAR DIARY
or
INTELLIGENCE SUMMARY

Army Form C. 2118

Place	Date	Hour	Summary of Events and Information	Remarks and references to Appendices
BEAUMETZ LES LOGES Sheet 51C Q23	1-4-17		Visited & inspected D.A.C. animals. H.Q. & Nos 1 & 2 Sections suffering badly still from exposure & frostbite & overwork. MVS evacuated 70 animals from BEAUMETZ STATION.	
	2-4-17		Visited AGNY & selected site for Mobile Collecting Post at M2 d.3.3. Inspected 164 & 168 Brigades. A shipment of horses in the afternoon & night. Very terrible for the animals which are mostly out in the open & 16 perished in the M.C.S. from exposure & exhaustion. Visited DAC. Found 8 dead horses also 6	
	3-4-17		293" AFA Bde & found 34 had died there from the same cause. Visited 260" & 281" RFA Bdes.	
	4-4-17		Visited 164" Bde & 16 Chuluzria at ACHICOURT & inspected them. 164" M.T. & 168 hrs from exposure, also suffering badly from the inclement weather.	
	5-4-17		Total sick 436. Invest sick 129. Died 166. Dest 53. Missing 0. Total strength.	
	6-4-17		Visited & inspected No1 Sect DAC & 2/3 of F.t. at GUOY. 9 Carabiniers Collecting Post at AGNY in afternoon.	
	7-4-17		Inspected No 16 A.S.C. & found 5 Mange Cases. DDVS 3rd Army visited my Office. VM Section	
	10-4-17		Started shipment of horses in afternoon & night. 12" Evacuated at GUOY.	
	11-4-17		V.O's Meeting in my Office. Evacuated again at GUOY. Total sick 312. Treat sick 137. Died 67 Dest 36	
	13-4-17		Missing 0. Total Strength 4644. 14" Marched to ACHICOURT. 16" Insp 163" Bde. 143 M.9 Co.	
ACHICOURT Sheet 51B M2 B24	14-4-17			
	16-4-17		MV Section Marched to AGNY to Aid of Collecting Post behind the Chateau.	
	17-4-17		Inspected 243 AFA Bde. & 281" RFA. 18" Insp DAC Nos 1 & 4 Sections & 167 TMB	

Army Form C. 2118

WAR DIARY
or
INTELLIGENCE SUMMARY.
(Erase heading not required.)

Instructions regarding War Diaries and Intelligence Summaries are contained in F.S. Regs., Part II. and the Staff Manual respectively. Title pages will be prepared in manuscript.

Place	Date	Hour	Summary of Events and Information	Remarks and references to Appendices
COUIN Sheet 57D J.1	19.4.17		Moved to COUIN with Div: live Artillery which I handed over to ADMS 30th Div:	
	20.4.17		Visited BRINCOURT & LABRET [sic] Automobile for MVS. Arrived in the later, also visited the stripping	
	20.4.17		Unit at LE GROSTISON FARM with a view to setting its arrangements, the train & 1/5 Cheshires & 165 MGC	
			Regts Total Sick 266. Trench Sick 64. Died 17. Admt 28. Missing 0. Total Strengths 4491	
	21.4.17		Visited LABRET to establish MVS there & LE GROSTISON FARM again.	
	23.4.17		Visited Hospital 10g Field. 193 M.G.Co. 92. 213 F.A.s. 575 Fld RE & No 4 Co A.S.C. 2 many cases in later.	
	24.4.17		Arrangements for stripping cancelled & orders for division to move back to been received.	
			Returned to DDMS & MO of Division before departing to front. Average about 5%	
HAUTEVILLE Sheet 51C J.30	24.4.17		Moved to HAUTEVILLE	
	25.4.17		Visited FREVENT at 9 a.m. with DA+QMG to inspect 140 Renewals arriving by Infantry Division	
	26.4.17		Visited ARRAS to establish MVS. Includes 112. 9th Div 19. Nu 3 M.S.B. Total Strength 1930.	
	27.4.17		Moved to ARRAS. Hy offices at No ?11 Rue de la Paix. 30 MV Section moved to ARRAS.	
ARRAS Sheet 51B 9.21	29.4.17		General remarks on evacuation. Much improved. Receipts 167th Inf. Brig 4/2/17. A.	

Major I. ?? ??
ADMS 56th Div.

Vol 15

Confidential
War Diary
of
56th Division
A.D.V.S.
From May 10th 1917
To May 31st 1917.

Army Form C. 2118.

WAR DIARY
or
INTELLIGENCE SUMMARY.
(Erase heading not required.)

Instructions regarding War Diaries and Intelligence Summaries are contained in F. S. Regs., Part II. and the Staff Manual respectively. Title pages will be prepared in manuscript.

Place	Date	Hour	Summary of Events and Information	Remarks and references to Appendices
ARRAS Sheet 71B G.21	1-5-17		Inspected 167 & 168 Rides. 164 in a bad way ununtilated especially of Middleset. 168 Satisfactory	
	2-5-17		except Dunbar Section which however are improved & 1774 9 Co. which is still unsatisfactory. Inspected 2, 3, & 4 Coy A.S.C. No. 2 Ry Groups 3 & 4 much improved. Ammunition 2/2 & 2/3 F.A.	
	" "		4 Coy ammunition 4/2 Group 4/3 fair. Capt H & Anthony were killed about 10.45 p.m.	
	" "		whilst asleep in his tent in the M.V.S. by a bomb dropped by an enemy aeroplane.	
	3...		Took over charge of M.V.S. pending appointment of successor to Capt H & Anthony.	
	" "		Inspected No. 612 & 513 FIELD Co R.E. all satisfactory & generally improved.	
	4...		164 Rde Gpers. Blew 15 shrapnel which have improved much. Freshly relieved	
	" "		batteries to transfer 45 Bde. 1 destroyed 3. Sand through 1 Bde. 40 Runsmede	
	5...		arrived in transit on 2-5-14 but they would be saved were recommandforward by Capt O'Brien R.E.	
	" "		Visited Army & Divisional Ammunition No 6 A S E & 281 Rde with Capt-Townsend. Satisfactory.	
	6...		Visited Heavy & inspected 250 Battery on. Satisfactory except that the ammunition strength	
	" "		Capt-Townsend took over charge of M.V.S. & Capt H. Hill ammunition & has 26 Pales who	
	7...		Capt Townsend appointed LTM.k. 11 having H.O.'s in my office. Freshly ammunition :-	
	" "		Total Rds 64 Shrap Rds 30 Did 0 Accompany Dud Strength 1809.	
	11...		Inspected whole division & Mounted Personnel Lt O'Driscoll Staff Learning march :- 4 Middlesex	
	14.9&16.		Attended meeting of A D & R's at A D D R S & Hts AVESNES LE COMPTE	Inspection Major
	15...			Lt/Ks & Bde

WAR DIARY
or
INTELLIGENCE SUMMARY.
(Erase heading not required.)

Army Form C. 2118.

Place	Date	Hour	Summary of Events and Information	Remarks and references to Appendices
ARRAS	16.5.17		"Robert Coy" 1 Middlesex still unsatisfactory. Management generally wanting. 168 M.G. Coy equipment unsatisfactory. 41 Field Ambulance. Barracks dirty 2/3 Infantry Hospital form.	
Maroeuil B	18.5.17		Meeting MOs in my office. Medley Returnee. Int. Rick to Inf. Brunchly Med Work. Little strength to be	
C. 21	19.5.17		Inspd. Y/D La R.F.A. 15" Div; One battery C any train TMO not being supported by O/C Bde in his treatment. This brought up. Insptd. 71st Fld Amb 4 in A battery TMand "Coront Throphie" Marg.	
	" "		20" Inspected 15" Div D.A.C. good. 21 Division moved to WARLUS.	
WARLUS	23 "		Examined by Remounts: H Division moved to HABARC. 26" Medly HO's in my office.	
Maroeuil B			Motor Veterinary Section moved to AGNEZ LES DUISANS on 21-5-17.	
HABARC	25 "		Probly Veterinary Insp Lich 25 Inmount Lick 9 Transpt Inspection 1 R.W.3 Reg. a little Unsatisfactory 1790	
	24 "		Inspected 168 Bde M.G. Coy still unsatisfactory + another heavy roll Inversion went. Alley 4th A.	
	26 "		Insp of Remounts 30. Inspd. Bde Remounts. Riding horse mange. 30 Insp by Rosd 2/17	
	" "		2/10 F.J. Neither Satisfactory. But slightly improved. 31 Inspected 62 Remounts. Lame	
	" "		& action Sufficient in 1 L.D. horses. Recondition attend to day. Les Herrick in disturbance	

Assistant Major JAKS 8/3 Nov.

Vol 16

Confidential
War Diary
of
A.D.S. 1st Division
From June 1st 1917

WAR DIARY or INTELLIGENCE SUMMARY

Army Form C. 2118

Place	Date	Hour	Summary of Events and Information	Remarks and references to Appendices
HABARC Sht-47C K8	1-6-17		Meeting of A.D.'s in my office. Weekly returns. Total sick 45. Transf. sick 25. Died 0. Total 1190	
	2-7-17		Inspected 168 M.A. Co. Found 5 sunfiring. Mange cases. Pequement factory, the Cavalier otherwise much	
	3 " "		Attended a meeting of A.D.V.S at D.D.V.S' office at AVESNES-LES-COMPTE. Transport Horses, H. Team	
	4 " "		Inspected No.8 Co. R.V. Train. Very good. 4. Attended reviews at NOYELLES-VION + GIVENCHY-LES-NOBLES.	
	5 " "		Sprained A.D.V.S + D.D.R. 16 M.V.S. for inspection. 10's meeting at my office.	
	" "		Weekly Returns - Total Sick 48. Transf. Sick 23. Destroyed 1. Died 0. Total strength 1863.	
ARRAS Sht-51B G.21	9 " "		To ARRAS to interview A.D.V.S 61st Div. He taking over. 15th Moved to ARRAS via GOUY-COURT L.	
	11 " "		Knocked to Rest with water trough used by an infected guardsman unit 151st H.A. Saw the	
	" "		Command Offr. Pulled down trough. Wrote Board to say no means could be seriously damaged in these Rd and stand.	
	" "		Mules brought in. Found still Sick 61st this Div. Who had been returned as unit had A.S.C.	
	" "		And 1st Another + Written to H.Q. Better instructions are but would not expect such.	
	12 " "		Inspected A.D.V.S 3rd Div 42 M.V.S Horse agreements much	
	" "		Inspected 163rd H. M.V.C still around suspicious skin cases. Lt Mac A.D.V.S II Corps	
	14 " "		ACHICOURT. H. arrangements made with 10th Brigade, Snatched 17 Brigade.	
	15 " "		Inspected 260th Bde R.F.A. V.O's much at my office. Indents 1 Div. 105 R.F.A.	
	" "		WEEKLY STRENGTHS RETURNS. Total sick 49. Transf. Sick 22. Died 2. Dest 8. Total strength 4032	

Robert Major
A.D.V.S II Corps

Army Form C. 2

WAR DIARY
or
INTELLIGENCE SUMMARY.
(Erase heading not required.)

Instructions regarding War Diaries and Intelligence Summaries are contained in F. S. Regs., Part II. and the Staff Manual respectively. Title pages will be prepared in manuscript.

Place	Date	Hour	Summary of Events and Information	Remarks and references to Appendices
ARRAS Sh.51B G.21	18.6.17		Inspected [?] bts 1st + 3rd Rdn RFA. Capt Staples returned in short hours to Ireland.	
	19		Insp 1/6g Rdn + 1/5 Cheshires. 20th Insp d Nor Sec. 12th DAC. 22nd Insp 138 A. Tr. 1/3 M.G. Co.	
			V.O's meeting in my office. Weekly Returns. S.I.T. sick 64 trans. Sick 39 Died 1 Med Trt [?]	
	23		Insp Nos. 2, 3, 4 + 6 + C.5 56 Div train Tot 52 F.C. RE 94 Insp 513 F.C. RE 2/1 7.4 1 25 [?]	
	25		Insp Cavalry Insp 2/3 F.A. 26th Insp 415 Fd Co RE + 2/2 + A.	
	28		Transfered Gen Stuell on his inspection of the [?] Mrs. 29th Svn inspected 2, 3 + 4	
	29		Cav + Australian [?]. Noy C. aw Asst Censor jotten [?]. V.O's meeting in my	
			office. Weekly Returns. S.I.T sick 64 trans. Sick 55 Died 0 Med 0 Abst O. Total Strength 3063	

[signature] J.M.K.S Lt Col

NE 17

Confidential
War Diary
of 1st Division
A.E.F.
From July 1st 1914
to July 31st 1914

WAR DIARY
or
INTELLIGENCE SUMMARY

Army Form C. 2118

Place	Date	Hour	Summary of Events and Information	Remarks and references to Appendices
ARRAS Shw7678	2.7.17		Inspected AWS & 165 M.G. Co	
G 21	4.7.17		March 16 LE CAUROY with Div: HQ	
LE CAUROY	6.7.17		Insp: 2/2 London F.A. Ambce Sick & Reinsp 5 Insp 2 63 Ramp: from PREVENT Reevacuation also No 4 Co Div: Train	
LENS 11	6.7.17		Insp Sick 47 Trans Pick S. Sick o No 4 Co Sick through 17 AA	
	8.7.17		WEEKLY RETURNS Latr Sick 47 Trans Pick-up	
	9.7.17		Insp 1/12 London (Rangers) H.Q. 5 M.G. Co 2/68 Bde H.Q. Lines	
	10.9.17		Insp: An IEA Transport with Col 6 Grant & Gubbins also all th. Chatteau in Nw	
	11.7.17		No: (see RFA) 11 Insp 1/3 M.G. Co 11 London & 1/4 Co Div Train	
	12.7.17		Insp 1/5 London (LRB) 19 London, 1/5 Cheshire & 3 Co R.E. (ref: +12-+513)	
			V.O.S. working by my 17 A. WEEKLY RETURNS Lst to Lst 38 Trans Sick 10 Died 1	
	13.7.17		Rev'd - Letter with Insp: 18 47 13 Insp: 164 London 1/1 London (WR) 1/16	
			(QVR) No4 Co Div Train + 2/2 London F.A.	
	14..		Attended meeting at DAD SUS 4 ADUS 3 then Trip to BRETEN COURT	
			Capt FR STAPLES NYC F. Evacuated from there Lr to the 60th	
			Insp: 1/6 Bde 2/1 London F.A. 3/1 No 2 Co Div Train	
	16..		Insp: H.Q. Div: & H.Q. Div. Train Transport with Col Grant & Morris	
	17..		Reviewed No 2 Co Div Train for Morris Insp: 19 Lond 1/ Berkshire Lond 16 London	
	18..			

WAR DIARY
INTELLIGENCE SUMMARY

Army Form C. 2.

Place	Date	Hour	Summary of Events and Information	Remarks and references to Appendices
LE CAUROY	19-7-17		t 3/16 c RE 116 572 + 570	
LENS	" "		WEEKLY RETURNS TOTAL SICK 111 transfd sick to ADS 0 OWS. Treatmt/mist 57.	
	20 " "		Insp. 119 London (AVR) 116 (QMR) 113 Border FA No 46 + 113 36 A.C.U. Train.	
	21 " "		Completed reports + form N.Q.	
EPERLECQUES	22 " "		Moved to EPERLECQUES. 24 MVs moved to EPERLECQUES.	
HAZEBROUCK	26-27-28		Insp. DivHd. Sqdn. 164 Bde. 2.3.4 G.S Train. 193 MGC 1/5 Chesh. 1/4 of 2/3 F.A. 91/7 MGC.	
SA	26		V.Os meeting in my OHrs. 28 wounded meeting ADVS officer 3 Corps	
	"		WEEKLY RETURNS. Sick & list 43 Transfd sick 10 No. 2 + No. 1 Aust. 1 British Remts. 1645.	
	30		Insped Pln Stores No. 2 Stables with ADVS V Corps.	
	31		Insp 1/2 Bde. 167 Bde + 416 & 417 RE.	
	31-7-17			

My G. Cameron
Maj AVS 63 Div.

Vol 18

Confidential
War Diary
of
D.A.D.S. 56th Canadian Division

From August 1-1917
to August 31-1917

WAR DIARY
or
INTELLIGENCE SUMMARY
(Erase heading not required.)

Army Form C. 2118

Place	Date	Hour	Summary of Events and Information	Remarks and references to Appendices
EPERLECQUES	2.8.14		[illegible handwritten entries]	
HAZEBROUCK 6A				
	3.6.14			
RENINGHELST	6.8.14			
SHEKAS G.26.8.yd				
	9.8.14			
	10.8.14			
	11.8.14			
	15.8.14			

Army Form C. 21.

WAR DIARY
or
INTELLIGENCE SUMMARY.
(Erase heading not required.)

Instructions regarding War Diaries and Intelligence Summaries are contained in F. S. Regs., Part II. and the Staff Manual respectively. Title pages will be prepared in manuscript.

Place	Date	Hour	Summary of Events and Information	Remarks and references to Appendices
RENINGHELST	16.8.17		Nearly returns unitary and 3/1 Field Amb 3/3 M.G. Coy to VIII Corps	13-RFA 17 RFA
Sheet 28	17/8/17		Insp. Nos. 1, 2, 3 + 4 Gmp A.S.C. 18 DDvS exam. reinf. transferred to Lads and DWS 1/3 WR	1/3 WR
G.19.c.4.d.	18/8/17		War Diary	
	19.8.17		Rec'd A.M. Inspected 3/1 N.F.L. Fd Amb 3/1 + 3/1 W.R 3 Durham Lt Inf	
			Insp'd A. Brigade — 2 Section 1/3 Fd Amb 18 RA — Lad V.R Adjutant 1/3 RFA 5 Durham	
	21.8.17		Worry not chain Rev'd	& Worcester Ambulance Reinforcements + N—	
	22.8.17		L. Proven 3/1 Sm E Sy Newmarket what a amount enhancing it. 3 new Billetts. (I was at & G.—	
EPERLECQUES A.13.87			Moved L'Eperlecques. Rec'd Cav S. Troop.	
HAZEBROUCK			War Diary Returns. Visited Div 3/3 Army 9/84 Aust 53 Nos. S. of the Mounted Bgde. (No. 16 H.S.T - A)	
STA			Capt Donnelly TC AVC admire d private of	
	24.8.17		Cap to H.Q. 100.K 30 Divn RFA Mornings on Shot + Gun 3 infantry. 20 Inspected 167 MG's	
	25.8.17		13 London 21 T.A. 15 Cheshires Signals 41GRE + 4A.S.C. 27 + 28 Exam wastes menin	
	26.8.17		in division in artillery with Corps Commander to Enquiry for Evening. Advised 16 + transfd. to	
	27.8.17		Weekly returns + 4 Fd Sick 151 Transfd sick + Died — Rev't Trial Strength 1933 (Annotations)	
FREMICOURT K.5	30-31		Moved to FREMICOURT LENS II KF	
LENS II	31-8-17		Mobile veterinary section arrived at FREMICOURT	Maj Caw Maj Ave TT DADVS K6 Division

31/8/17

Vol 19

Confidential

War Diary
of
D.A.D.V.S. 56th Division

from Sept. 16th 1914
to Sept. 30th 1914

Army Form C. 2118

WAR DIARY
or
INTELLIGENCE SUMMARY.
(Erase heading not required.)

Instructions regarding War Diaries and Intelligence Summaries are contained in F. S. Regs., Part II. and the Staff Manual respectively. Title pages will be prepared in manuscript.

Place	Date	Hour	Summary of Events and Information	Remarks and references to Appendices
FREMICOURT LENS II K.5	1-9-17		Rec'd wire from ADVS IV Corps Lt. Mm. M.V.S. Lt. ROCQUIGNY. Visited prepared site with O.C. M.V.S. & an A. vern in our opinion quite unsuitable. 1st because of the exposed position & 2nd because of the distance from water. Asked to retain site at FREMICOURT. Inspected 2/1 F.A. at BATASTRE.	
	2-9-17		Insp'd 165 Inf'y Bde, 193 M.G. Coy & 2/2 F.A.	
	3-9-17		Visited ADVS IV Corps wk OC. Notice that CAPT WOLFE had been ordered to join for duty wh OC Motor Ac ROCQUIGNY onto but was ordered to occupy it & prepare it would stand by. Army M.V.S. Kennels	
	4-9-17		Rec'd notice that CAPT HEANEY had been nominated for Army duty. Two M.V.S. Went Insp'd 164 Bde 15- Cheshires & 2/3 F.A. 5th Insp'd 250 Field RFA DAC M.O. ASC. & AV trooks HQ- Insp'd 2/5 Field RFA all pts except D which in dubiously Arid. Meeting of HO's hit only announced to attend.	
	5-		CAPT deWOLFE Arr'd T.C. arrived & detailed for duty vice CAPT HEANEY evacuated sick. CAPT J.HILL	
	6-		returned to duty from leave & attended Conference at office of ADVS IV Corps. 10" Insp'd A.T.D/287 RFA Insp'd 250 F'd RFA A Battery not satisfactory. Insp'd 10. 93- Very good C. Arty D good	
	11-		Insp'd D.A.C. Good. 12- Insp'd RFA with ADS 3 Army & Hdrs IV Corps. & RA.	
	-		Ex.2 of 94 Punjabis DAC animals at B Eschelon. June 22. V.O.s meeting in May off.	
	15-		Attended Conference at Office of ADVS IV Corps. CAPT WOLFE transferred to 3rd Div for duty.	
	16-		CAPT HEANEY Rec'd 1/2 duty from leave from hospital. Inspected 165- Inf Bde an autologus & 2/5 F.A.	
	17-		D.D.R. & ADS visited HQ & exam't read animals immediately for other troops removing removing	

M. JW deWay HTC
ADVS 61st Div

WAR DIARY
or
INTELLIGENCE SUMMARY.
(Erase heading not required.)

Army Form C. 2118.

Place	Date	Hour	Summary of Events and Information	Remarks and references to Appendices
FREMICOURT	14.9.17		Cast 22 for review on parade. Also sent 18 for veterinary exam. All three were severely lame & refused till the DAC would not on shortening of establishment.	
LENS II	15 "		Insp of HQ horses & of Insp of Rds. W.I.1 ford. Selected two horses from 25 Bde for reposturation.	
K b"	16 "		Insp of HQ horses & of Insp of Rds. W.I.1 ford. Selected two horses from DAC for reposturation.	
	18 "		CAPT HEANEY went on short leave to Ireland. (Left me in Maj) CAPT H. KIRK arrived for duty.	
	" "		Nil CAPT DONNELLY ordered to join the 51st Divn. Insp of W.R.E. Cos & 2/3 F.A. all good. veigh - 672 lbs	
	19 "		Had a Report mare from 250 Bde for reposturation. 25 Corps IV Commander inspected all the above mentioned. Mare accepted & branded 5 T. V. O's meeting in my office in afternoon.	
	20 "		Insp of HQ Rds (6 Mx & 1 Wilts Jntry) 198 M.G. Co. MT guns. NWF guns approved and assumed of dy nails only fair.	
	21 "		CAPT DONNELLY away. Attended Conference on ADVS Office n 1 IV Corps. 13 French arrived NM pm	
	22 "		5 Remts arrived, nat very good. Can't 3 for Reinforcement Stability. Insp Hq & No 3 Co A.S.C. & 1 Cheshire good.	
	23 "		Visited men home standing the A utility unit & AA & M G. & 1 Cheshire.	
	24 "		Insp stable of RFA horses & Standings with G.O.C., C.R.A & A.H. & M.G. Insp of Rds & horses in afternoon.	
	25 "		V. O's meeting in my office.	
	26 "		29 Inspected 16 Bde with G.O.C Insp Rds & three abominable IV Corps - principal fault black if appearing & being indifferent. Forges badly required in his opinion.	
	29 "			

30 - 9 - 17

Yr Hectr Maj DVS
WANVS 62nd Div

WD 20

Confidential
War Diary
of
16th Division
D.A.Q.M.S.
From October 1st 1917
to October 31st 1917

Original

WAR DIARY or INTELLIGENCE SUMMARY

Army Form C. 2118

Instructions regarding War Diaries and Intelligence Summaries are contained in F.S. Regs., Part II. and the Staff Manual respectively. Title pages will be prepared in manuscript.

(Erase heading not required.)

Place	Date	Hour	Summary of Events and Information	Remarks and references to Appendices
FREMICOURT LENS XI K 5	1.10.17		Visited DAC Coxer. 17 Remounts. Pow Lt. Capt Heaney returned from leave. Insp'd horses of 2/c 8th Lond: F.A. All very good except 2 which are old & in poor condition.	
	2 "		Inspected 11 animals of 193 M.G.C. for overseas. Insp: 281 Bde RFA. Good except 1 battery which still have animals at D.A.C. Good. 4" Capt C W Townsend proceeded on 16 days leave to England. Insp: 250 Bde RFA C/251 arrived from horse standing good. V.O's conference in my office.	
	3 "			
	4 "		Total Strength Sick 97 Insani. Sick 8 Died 1 Destroyed 1 Total Strength 3953.	
	5 "		Supervised killing of 11 animals of 193 M.G. Co. + 11 of 167 M.G.Co. with Walker by Capt Burrell ANC No IV Corps.	
	6/7/6		Visited IV Corps L'tkra ADVS in absence of ADVS on leave, & Insp: 416, 512 + 613 "Co's RE & 43 Dvn d.i.T. A.	
	9 "		Insp: 169 Tde + B Echelon D.A.C. all good. 10 Insp: D.v Train all good except No 4 Co which has many poor thin horses the rest good with their animals if clipping. Insp: HQ DIV. CRE CRA all good. Also 1+2 & 3 J. D.A.C. very good.	
	10 "			
	11 "		V.O's Conference in my office. Total Sick 109 Trans: Sick 19 Died 1 Dest 0 Total Strength 4140	
	11 "		Insp: 164 Bde. 1/8 Middx much improved. Radgood. 13 Insp: 1/4 N Staffs newly arrived with 55 horses. Poor.	
	13 "		Attended conference of offrs of ADVS IV Corps. 14 Insp: 1/5 Cheshires very good. 15 Insp: 36 Co RE + 2/3 Bde FA.	
	16 "		Insp: 169 Bde. Very good. Y 193 M.G.Co. Much jumping in evidence. 17 Insp: 250 + 251 Bdes R.F.A. D/251 still very unsatisfactory. Many thin. Harness dirty. Horses. 18 Insp: B Echelon DAC & horses. Middex station very good.	
	19		V.O's meeting in my office. Total Sick 111 Trans: Sick 24 Died - Destroyed 2. Total Strength. 4064	

Army Form C. 2118

WAR DIARY
or
INTELLIGENCE SUMMARY.
(Erase heading not required.)

Instructions regarding War Diaries and Intelligence Summaries are contained in F.S. Regs., Part II. and the Staff Manual respectively. Title pages will be prepared in manuscript.

Place	Date	Hour	Summary of Events and Information	Remarks and references to Appendices
FREMICOURT LENS XI K 6	19-10-17		Insp^d Div: train. No 4 Co much imp^d. Rest good especially No 1 & No 2 Co's.	
	20.10.17		Attended Conference at HQrs ADVS IV Corps.	
	23-10-17		B A D V S proceeded on leave to England (Dates 28/10/17 to 8/11/17)	
	25-10-17		Capt J. HILL AVC. Acting B A DVS. V.Os on leave at Fmg office. Total sick 976. Transfd sick 6. Died Nil.	
			Destroyed 5. Total Strength 4109	
	27-10-17		Attended Conference at office of A.D.V.S. Corps.	
	28-10-17		D.V.S. and accompanied by MAJOR VALLEY A.V.C. in attendance D.D.V.S. Third Army & A.D.V.S. IV Corps. visited Hd Qrs Mot Vet Section. 50 Remounts arrived for Division, including about 4 very poor nags which were returned to Standard.	

November 1st 1917

Austin Capt AVC
Acting B ADVS 62 Division

Jul 21

Confidential

War Diary
of
50th Division

Nov. 31st 1917.

G.A.D.S.
Loc IIIst Edn M.F.
Gen.
Nov 1st 1917.

Original

WAR DIARY
or
INTELLIGENCE SUMMARY.

(Erase heading not required.)

Army Form C. 211

Place	Date	Hour	Summary of Events and Information	Remarks and references to Appendices
FREMICOURT	1-11-17	-	V.O's conference at office of D.A.D.V.S. TOTAL SICK 110 TRANSFERRED SICK 14, DIED 1, DESTROYED NIL, TOTAL STRENGTH 4086.	
SHEET LENS 11, SQUARE K5	5-11-17	-	Attended Conference at office of A.D.V.S. Examined a scabing taken from 4th Horse of 7th Coy 56 Divisional train. PSOROPTIC PARASITE was found. Due precautions were taken and disinfector carried out. Affected animals evacuated.	
	8-11-17		V.O. conference at office of DADVS. TOTAL SICK 115 TRANSFD SICK 29. DIED NIL DESTROYED NIL, TOTAL STRENGTH 4082. MAJOR W. ASCOTT. A.V.C. returned from leave today.	
	10-11-17		Attended Conference at office of ADVS IV Corps.	
	12-11-17		Visited 512 R E Coy 6 Amps; Cases of Mange. Examined scrapings. No acari found. Sent to L&H TWS for treatment. Last Mons scrapings taken with Negative but examined. All precaution taken in brand 3 Cases Surgt Mange at Signal Co. Scrapings negative but evacuated.	
	13-11-17		Action Mange (mostly seasonal) is responsible in these for the recent cases.	
	14-11-17		CaptKirk left in evening for 14 days leave to England. 15th CaptKirk recalled by other V/ADVS IV Corps. V.O's conference in my office.	
	15-11-17		Attended Conference at Q office re Prospect in operations.	
	15-11-17		TOTAL SICK 98 TRANSFERRED SICK 9 DIED NIL DESTROYED 4 TOTAL STRENGTH 4053.	
	16-11-17		Visited LEBUCHIERE with DADVS 62 Div. to advise re of the cutter of Prob. Scabies & Mange.	

W. Jacum Maj: DADVS, 6th Div.

WAR DIARY
or
INTELLIGENCE SUMMARY.

Army Form C. 2118

Place	Date	Hour	Summary of Events and Information	Remarks and references to Appendices
FREMICOURT Shell LENS 11 S.K.2"	15.11.17		1½ "Reveille" arrived at D.A.C. Officers & Others Conference re ADMS IV Corps. My duties prevented in short leave to England	
	16.11.17		62" Div: MVS arrived at 11.30 a.m.: MVS + 2 mules with him during operations	
	17.11.17		Officers Conference at Office of ADVS IV Corps.	
	18.11.17		CAPT KIRK R.E. from leave being recalled. Advices for transfer to other units & evacuation 25 Amphine animals from 56 Div train.	
	20.11.17		Established advanced collecting post w- the Gres Verdo LEBUCQUIERE. Personnel 1 Corpl + 1	
			Private of the 62 Div MVS + 2 privates from 11 divl MVS. 22 V.O's meeting in my office.	
	22.11.17		Total Sick 115 Transferred Sick 25 Died 1 Destroyed 2 Total Strength 4045	
	24.11.17		6 horses killed + 3 wounded by shell fire belonging to A/281st de R.F.A. Attended at ADVS IV Corps for conference. W.A. held at supposition	
			22 10 " " +4 " " " " " " " D/280 " " " " " Wagon lines	
			" 6 " " +3 " " " " " " " " " " " " Divisional train	
	25.11.17		" 10 " " +2 injured " " well drawn down by gale in 109/281 Bde wagon lines	
	27.11.17		Visited ADVS & Corps Vet depot. 22" V.O's meeting in my office	
	29.11.17		Total Sick 164 Transferred Sick 26 Died 33 Destroyed 3 Total Strength 3985	
				Maj. J. Scott. Muir. D.A.D. V.S. 62 Div.

DADVS.
November 29, 1917.

Vol 22

Confidential
War Diary
of
D.A.D.V.S. 56th (London) Division

From December 1st/17
to December 31st/17

Original

Army Form C. 2118.

WAR DIARY
or
INTELLIGENCE SUMMARY.
(Erase heading not required.)

Instructions regarding War Diaries and Intelligence Summaries are contained in F. S. Regs., Part II. and the Staff Manual respectively. Title pages will be prepared in manuscript.

Place	Date	Hour	Summary of Events and Information	Remarks and references to Appendices
FREMICOURT				
Ahead] LENS II	1.12.17		Attended Conference in office of ADVS VI Corps. Withdrew Advanced Collecting Part from LEBUCHERE.	
Sqn K 5	3.12.17		Mobile Vet: Section bombed by aircraft about 2.30 a.m. 4 bombs dropped 4 a hut, damaged hut, no casualties except 1 Corpl of the 62nd Div. MVS wounded & removed to a/c F.A. O/c very narrow escape. Lieut Kirk proceeded	
3Hy[Lens II Sy C3 FOSSEAUX	5.12.17		Moved to FOSSEAUX. A/c its Mobile Vet: Section holiday. Reported to ADVS XIII Corps at ECOIVRE	
VICTORY CAMP ROCLINGCOURT	4.12.17 6.12.17		Visited DADVS of 31st Div: he being over. 5th Moved to VICTORY CAMP ROCLINGCOURT. MVS to ANZIN Gy [tpdr 1/19]	
			Met ADVS XIII Corps at MVS at ANZIN. 1st Total Sick. 42. Trans: Sick 5. Died Nil. Destroyed 3. Total Strength 2148	
Ahead 151 B/W	8.12.17		Visited Emp 416. 512 & 513 R.E. Cas. 512 Emp? Others 2 Gord. Also 198 M.G. Co. Gord. & Signal Co. Fair.	
G 3 b	9.12.17		Emp 164 Inf: Fld Transport: Pale animals with ADVS XIII Corps. Satisfactory except HQ which is poor.	
	11.12.17		Emp Div Train with ADVS XIII Corps. Everything Nor So not yet arrived. No 2 Gord. No 3 Pow Nor 4 Fair.	
	12.12.17		Attended Conference at office of ADVS XIII Corps. he new orders re Specific Ophthalmia	
	13.12.17		Emp 166 & 4 Pk. Ple Transport animals with ADVS XIII Corps. 115 V.G. 112 113 Gord Hy Section Pow.HQ Gord MG Gord Fair	
	14.12.17		Emp 21 F.A at AUBIGNY.] Total Sick 42. Trans Sick 14. Died 1. Destroyed 2. Total Strength 3955. (Ophthalmia 13)	
	15.12.17		Emp 169 Lgt Fld Transp: animals with ADV S XII Corps. All Gord. Also Emp Div H.Q + 2/3 F.A. Gord	
	16.12.17		Visited Hosp 260 Rde RFA. Collected from Ave Hummead 1st 6th Div: 216 Frames for Stationary and thereafter to ADVS XIII Corps	
	17.12.17		Lieut W.H. KIRK M.C. from leave 18.12.17 Capt J. MILL proceeded on leave to England. Insp. 251 Rde RFA.	
	19.12.17		Visited XIII Corps to acting ADVS re St. Col. Gamble on leave. Insp. 16 Checking transport animals.	

31-12-17 [signature] Major DADVS VI Div.

Army Form C. 2118

WAR DIARY
or
INTELLIGENCE SUMMARY
(Erase heading not required.)

Place	Date	Hour	Summary of Events and Information	Remarks and references to Appendices
VICTORY CAMP ROLLINGCOURT Abt 65 A NW 9.3.6.	20-12-17		Inspected No. 1 Co. of 6th Div. Train. Very good. Visited XIII Corps on acting ADVS.	Ukrainian at 64.
	21-12-17		Inspected No. 3 Co. — Only fair. Total Sick 136. Transf Sick 20. Died 1. Dest. Nil. Total Strength 4042.	Ukrainian cases at 64.
	22-12-17		Visited XIII Corps ADVS Office. Examined Field M. Vetnus. 23rd Visited 3/1 FA at AUBIGNY.	
	24-12-17		" " " 25th Inspected B + D /251st RFA. 1 Can Mange + 4 Mistakuin.	
	26-12-17		" " " 27th Inspected 1/6 Ukrainien. 3 cases suspicious of Mange. Animals good.	
	27-12-17		V.O.'s meeting in my office. 28th Inspected Bn HQ animals HMMP. Slightly manufactured. Remaining very	
	28-12-17		Visited XIII Corps. Total Sick 128. Transf Sick 41. Died Nil. Destroyed Nil. Total Strength 4058. Wounded	
	29-12-17		Horse Cases Ukrainien at 12. 29th Visited XIII Corps ADVS Office.	
	30-12-17		Inspected Depot Co. 1 Ukrainien. Animals good. Visited XIII Corps ADVS Office.	
	31-12-17			

31-12-17

J Stuart Muir
ADMS 5th Div

D.A.D.V.S.,
56TH DIVISION.
No. 112/8
Date

Confidential
War Diary
of
56th Division
D.A.D.V.S.
From January 1st /18
To January 31st /18

Army Form C. 2118

WAR DIARY
or
INTELLIGENCE SUMMARY
(Erase heading not required.)

Instructions regarding War Diaries and Intelligence Summaries are contained in F.S. Regs., Part II. and the Staff Manual respectively. Title Pages will be prepared in manuscript.

Place	Date	Hour	Summary of Events and Information	Remarks and references to Appendices
VICTORY CAMP	1·1·18		To 1/1 London MVS. 2nd Do XIII Corps dipping bath. In inspection progress & works satisfactory progress.	
ROCLINCOURT Sheet 51B.NW G 5 b	2·1·18		Do XIII Corps dipping bath.	
	3·1·18		Inspected 51'o Div: HQ, Signals, CRE & CRA horses. All good. To ADVS office XIII Corps an ADVS V.O.'s meeting in my office. CAPT JOHN HILL A.V.C.T.F. rejoined from leave.	
	4·1·18		Inspected 1/1 London Batt: horses for draft to reinforce nigh Mange. Found rice. Snng.-MVS with DAQMG 51'o Div: TOTAL SICK 96 TRANS SICK 40 DIED — DESTROYED 1 TOTAL STRENGTH 4082. OPHTHALMIA RECORD TOTAL CASES #44 CURED 10 TRANSF TO BASE 28 REMAINING under TREATMENT 5/6. CAPT WITHEARLEY AVC proceeded to Ireland on leave.	
	5·1·18		Snng.- 281st FDe RFA A.B + D good. 109" V good. Found 9 Ophthalmia cases. Jo ADVS office Corps an ADVS.	
	6·1·18		To back area with DC 1/1 Lond: MVS to select a site for MVS. Selected at VANDELICOURT.	
	7·1·18		Snng.- 281st FDe RFA A good event— 2 andutition which were dirty. 23rd D. Good. G. Satisfactory.	
	8·1·18		Very heavy snow + wind. A regular blizzard + was unable to inspect any units in consequence.	
MINGOVAL Sheet 51b V 23 b	9·1·18		Moved to MINGOVAL. Mobile V.S. moved to VANDELICOURT. Visited ADVS office XIII Corps an ADVS.	
	10·1·18		Yeomanry. V.O's meeting in my office. ADVS XIII Corps met. 11th Command Kpn of trench area.	
	11·1·18		Inspected Transport Dines. Visited 1/1 London MVS with ADVS XIII Corps. TOTAL SICK 89 TRANS SICK 11 DIED — DEST 2 TOTAL STRENGTH. 3963. OPHTHALMIA. ADMITTED 32 CURED 10 TRANS 1 REM 22. TOTAL CASES 58	
	12·1·18		Cont'n Kpn of Trench area. 13·14·15" distr finishing inspection. Practically every standing was bad. Government attendance etc. few there who had been discharged or badly damaged. Civilian attendance very bad, + all in a filthy condition.	
	13,14,15			
	16·1·18		+17· Very heavy rain. 17" V.O. meeting in my office. 18" Insp 16" Cheshire. 16th mg. Div HQ & Signals. W.Nos 6 V & Nos 1 & 2.	

WAR DIARY
or
INTELLIGENCE SUMMARY
(Erase heading not required.)

Army Form C. 2118

Instructions regarding War Diaries and Intelligence Summaries are contained in F. S. Regs., Part II. and the Staff Manual respectively. Title Pages will be prepared in manuscript.

Place	Date	Hour	Summary of Events and Information	Remarks and references to Appendices
MINGOVAL Sheet 36 B V 25 b.	18.1.18		TOTAL SICK 90 TRANSF 5 REMG 14 TOTAL 40. CURED 17 TRANSF 6 REMG 14 TOTAL 40.	
	19.1.18		CAPT W H HEANEY AVC ret from leave. Insp 1/3 Ind: 280 Bde D.T.43. Good. A/281 T109. Good. No ½ train V good. Inspected H8 Remounts at GOUCHIN LEGAL. Found 1 care sarcoptic mange 1 Ringworm + 3 Opthalmia. Also found 4 cases of Sarcoptic mange in civilian animals at No 3 billet GAMBLIGNEUL	ADMITTED 12 CURED 16 TRANS 3 REM 15 TOTAL 34.
	20.1.18		With all necessary precautions to prevent spread gave instructions for treatment.	
	" "		Insp 193 M.G.C. QVR's 251/3 281/D No 4 Co T train 2/5 ¾ J.T. D.A.C. all satisfactory. Standing up improved.	
	21 " "		So Camouflaged with APM re mange in civilian horses. Insp 164 H Q & Gardens Battalion.	
	22 " "		AVC sergts examined & classified by ADMS. YA under 41 A under 41 Remainder B. Insp 211 ¾ A. Good.	
	23 " "		Capt C.W.TOWNSEND proceeded on leave to England. 24 Insp 164 HQ + ¾ Middlesex. Good. V.O's meeting in my office. Capt J. HILL reported that he had found 5 c.c. Saturated sol: of Iodine more successful injection into Opthalmia	
	24 " "		Insp 280/A + 280/C. Good. TOTAL SICK 100. TRANSF 15 DIED 1 DEST 2 TOT STRENGTH 4000. OPHTHALMIA adm 25	
	26 " "		CURED 17 TRANSF 6 REM 19 TOTAL 40. 26. Insp 16 Cheshire. Dul. 1 case of JA mm found 1 mange case, other good.	
	27 " "		Parade of horses for casting at FREVILLERS. Card 11 for Veterinary reasons. 28 Insp MVS. 1 Gardens. 169 MG Co. No ½ train	
	28 " "		all good. 168 MGC. Fair melting due to standing. 168 HQ, Ranger's Ind: sentish. Good.	
	29 " "		Insp No 2 too train (out in the open still) Remaining 2/5 ¾ A + 166 M G Co. all good. 30 Insp Div H Q + Signals good.	
	30 " "		Insp D.A.C. V.good. A lot of work has been done on standing. V.O's meeting in my office.	
	31 " "			

My Sheet: Mgr 6/Div : 1.2.18
A.D.S./S 6 Div : 1.2.18

1-2-18

Vol 24

Confidential
War Diary
of
56th (Coy) Division

D.A.D.W.S.
From February 1st 1918
to February 28th 1918

WAR DIARY
or
INTELLIGENCE SUMMARY

(Erase heading not required.)

Army Form C. 2118

Place	Date	Hour	Summary of Events and Information	Remarks and references to Appendices
MINGOVAL Sheet 36B V 23 b.	1-2-16		Total Sick 127 Trans 55 Died 1 Dest 2 Total Strength 3944 Opthalmia. Adm 18 1 Cured 5 Trans 19 Rem'd 11 Total 35	
	2-2-16		Insp'd 260 Bde RFA with CRA & DAQMG. A. Good q'ns Rcvd nurthering Itrchmwd. C. Good. R. Good but enemy lightning	
	3-2-16		Insp'd 169 MG.C.Coy. A. Good. + 2/c T.A. Good. 4" to MVS. 4 wounded Jermin cases in civilian hosp in the village	
	4-2-16		Met D ADVS 1 Army & ADVS XIII Corps at MVS.	
	6-2-16		Insp'd 281" Bde RFA & DAC with CRA. All good. 109" V Good. 4" Insp'd NN H.Q.Y. Signals.	
	8-2-16		Total Sick 89 Trans 11 Died 2 Dest'd O. Strength 3909. Opthalmia. Adm'd 6 Cured 4 Trans 1 Rem 10 Total 11	
	8-2-16		Insp'd 6 12" & Co RE + 1/13 London at Ecoivre. V Good. ADVS XIII Corps.	
VICTORY CAMP ROCLINGCOURT Sheet 51 & NW 12.2.16 G 3. b.	12.2.16		R/W: Arrived to Victory Camp Roclingcourt. 12" Major W. Accott. DADVS Arrived in leave	
	15.2.16		to England + Capt C.W. Townsend. D.O.I. MVS. W.R. are his duties during his absence.	
			Tot Sick 94. Trans 82. Died — Dest'd — Strength 4032. Opthalmia. Ad 14 11 Cured 6 Trans 11 Rem'd 9. Total 26	
	17.2.16		G.O.C.Div. Insp 167 Inf Bde & the acting DADVS attended inspection. 89 Runners arrived & were	
	" "		Ophthalmia'd + picked up nail amongst tress recommends. 2/ GOC Div Insp 16# Bde.	
	22.2.16		Tot Sick 84. Tr.Sick 22 Died Dest Strength 3904 Opthalmia. Ad 18 11 Cured 5 Trans 9. Rem 13. Total 24	
	23.2.16		GOC Div insp 169 Inf Bde + Capt Kirk attended thereto DADVS being at a conference at XIII Corps.	
	26.2.16		GOC Div insp 260 + 281 Bdes RFA the acting DADVS attended. 2/ DAC + 1/ Lnd MVS attn'd.	
	27.2.16		DADVS Insp'd from leave.	

(Sig) J.H. Brett. Maj: DADVS

1-3-16

Original 16

Vol 25

Confidential

War Diary
of
1st 56th (Lewis) Division

D.A.D.O.S.
from 1-3-15 -
2-5-15
9-4-15
to 30-18

WAR DIARY
or
INTELLIGENCE SUMMARY

(Erase heading not required.)

Army Form C. 2118

Place	Date	Hour	Summary of Events and Information	Remarks and references to Appendices
VICTORY CAMP ROCLINGCOURT Sheet 51b NW G.3.b.	1.3.18		Total Sick 44 Transferred Sick 16 Died — Destroyed 2 Total Strength 3901	
	2.3.18		Opthalmia. Rem: L Ret. 18 Adm? 10 Total 23. 11 Teams Evac: 2 Rem "under treat" N/12 Total 23	46
	3.3.18		Inspected Div. H.Q including M.M.P. V good except 2 team in M.M.P. D.J.C. Signals excepts-team-	
	4.3.18		Inspected 43 Renownds at M.V.S. 1 Roannuite 1 Ulceration + Debility (evac?) 1 Newcomer reported 4 team died en rout	
	5.3.18		Inspected 16 Cheshires. Good especially considering T.O. had not sufficient warm. 5 Insp. 4th Fd Amb. Good but	
	6.3.18		Mules require more supervision. Covered a stand at M.V.S. 4 exc. a A.D. of Signal Co. O/c MVS acted as N.O. in absence	
	7.3.18		Inspect 169 Inf Bde. as a whole very good. 2nd V.O's meeting in my office.	
	8.3.18		Attended contin.g parade held by DDR on the football ground at Stupney. Insp: 168 Suitable. Good.	
			Returns. Rem: L.R. 33 Adm? 42 Total Sick. 44/45 11 on Duty. 16 Evac. 5 Died 2 Dest - 11 Strength 3925- 10 Mar': 18	
	8.3.18		Started Dipping trials at G.Biii Copse Bethany Park, ECURIE. Arrangrts for 6 animals per hour for 4 hours = 420	
			Inspect - A.S.C. unit O/c Team Nos. 1 + 2 Cos. V.G. except: Poultice cases in Nos. N/o + 2. Good. No. 3 Fair	
			Continued dipping Insp: 2/1 Can: Field Amb: Good. Visited 169 Debris etc at Roclingcourt.	
	9.3.18		Opthalmia Returns. Rem: L.R. 12. Adm? 4 Total 19 11 on Duty. 5 Evac. - Rem: under Treat. 14 Total 14.	
	10.3.18		Continued dipping of horses but improved rate to 70 per hour + finished at 2 p.m. horses allotted. Total 1260	
			As result of experience gained believe 100 per hour could be safely arranged for in any weather and—	
			Since there was of dip will not suit with 60 per hour to allow for any stoppage (unforeseen)	
	11. " " "		Inspected 169 M.G.Co. with D.M.G.O. Only fair. Consider supervision not good.	
			W. Meent Maj. DADV 58 Div	

Army Form C. 2118

WAR DIARY
or
INTELLIGENCE SUMMARY
(Erase heading not required.)

Instructions regarding War Diaries and Intelligence Summaries are contained in F. S. Regs., Part II. and the Staff Manual respectively. Title Pages will be prepared in manuscript.

Place	Date	Hour	Summary of Events and Information	Remarks and references to Appendices
ANZIN G.S.c.35 Sheet 51bNW	12.3.18		Owing to VICTORY CAMP being continuously shelled moved office to the Mill House ANZIN with ADMS & APM	
	14 " "	"	Attended conference of DADsVS at office of ADVS XIII Corps to discuss possible reduction of equipment. No VOSmeeting held	
	15 " "	"	RETURNS. Ad^d H6 Total Sick 87 || To Duty 24 Evac 23 Died 0 Dest 1. Rem^d H1. || Strength 3946. Wastage ⁶⁰/₀·⁷.	
	"	"	OPTHALMIA. Rem: L.R. 14, A.d-g 12, Total 26 || To Duty 18 || Rem^d under Krishnar Op. Total H26	
	18 " "	"	Attended inspection of animals of 3rd Indian Rangers & QVR (Divisional Battalion) by DDR. Inspected Lr. Remounts, 2 Opthalmia.	
	19 " "	"	Insp^d 167th Bn^s 6th^e Rde & 56th M.G.A. All good. 20° Insp^d 28th Bde RFA All good. 21st Ditto 280th Bde.	
	22 " "	"	Attended Conference of DADsVS at 1st army with A.G.V.S. at LILLERS.	
	" "	"	RETURNS. Rem^d H1. Adm 22. Total Sick 60 || To Duty 18 Evac 4 Died 1 Dest 1. Rem^d 39 || Strength 3963. Wastage ⁶⁰/₀·15.	
	23 " "	"	OPTHALMIA. Rem: L.R. 9 Ad^d 9 Total 18 || To Duty 4 Evac 1 Rem^d under treatment 13 Total	
	25 " "	"	CAPT J.R. CONCHIE AVC.TF, reported for duty to relieve CAPT W.H.KIRK.AVC.TF, & 26 CAPT W.H.KIRK. AVC.TF,	
	26 " "	"	proceeded to England for duty on conscientious grounds. Inspected 56th Div.M.G. Batt. animals. All good.	
	" "	"	Inspected H16th 512th & 513th Coys R.E. All good. 28th Moved to AGNIERES. 29 MVS moved to AGNIERES leaving	
AGNIERES Sheet 51c E.9.c.1.1.	28 " "	"	a collecting post at ANZIN pending arrival of relieving division MVS.	
	29 " "	"	RETURNS Ad^d 26 Total Sick 66 || To Duty 22 Evac 21 Died - Dest 2. Rem^d 20 || Strength H035 Wastage 15/₀.	
	" "	"	OPTHALMIA Returns. Adm 3. Total 16 || To Duty 10 Evac. 6 Rem^d under Treat^t Nil Total 16.	

W. J. Trevor Major
DADVS 56th Div.

31/3/18

WO 236

17
Original

Confidential

War Diary
of 1st Bn Khaiber Rifles

O.C. 1st Bn Khaiber Rifles
From April 1st 1918
to April 30th 1918

Army Form C. 2118.

WAR DIARY
or
INTELLIGENCE SUMMARY.
(Erase heading not required.)

Place	Date	Hour	Summary of Events and Information	Remarks and references to Appendices
AGNIERES E.2.C.1.1. Sheet 57C	1-4-18		Examined 53 Reinnard at Vacuelette on Mont St Eloi. 2 Ophthalmia & 1 Blind both eyes. At how lot. Insp M.G. Battalion. Men good. About 7 per horses. Insp 4th & 13th Infantry Regtl. horses, each good.	
	2-4-18		Recd. correspondence re neglect of duty by Cpl. J.R. Conchie A.V.C. T.F. whilst attached to 42nd Division & in accordance with instructions currently recommending to demand to make a further statement in his own defence as he did not consider he had a proper opportunity of so doing. Forwarded this statement with the correspondence relating to the matter.	
	3- " "		Insp 167th & Q Minnie. Good. 7th Middlesex. 9. 8th Middlesex in training.	
	4- " "		Nil.	
	6- " "		including MMP. All good except 2 MP. Horses	
	8- " "		too sprained. No NCO in charge. Stables & manure generally dirty but the lines in good condition.	
			Returns Rgt 20 A 46 Total 66 // Cured 11 Evac 8 Died 7 Dest 3 Rgt 36 Total 66 // Strength 4031 Wastage 4%	
			OPHTHALMIA Rgt 1 A 3 Total 4 // Cured 1 Evac — Rem 3	
	6- " "		To 17th Corps Area re Army wounded etc. V.O's meeting in Army H Que. Inspect Slaughter Transport. Satisfactory.	
BERNEVILLE a6d 79 Sheet 57C WARLUS K 36.6.5.7. Sheet 57C	8- " "		Aw: HQ moved to WARLUS & BERNEVILLE. My offices opened at BERNEVILLE Q6479	
	" "		Nil; Insp MVS moved to MONTENESCOURT. 2" ADVS XIII Corps visited re current arrangements	
	10- " "		moved to No 1 Camp WARLUS — 11" Visited MVS & DAC. V.O's meeting in any office.	
	12- " "		Inspect MMP. Good & 291st RFA. A & B Good. 109 Kingpost D Trin. much improved	
			Returns Rgt 36 A 28 Total 64 // Cured 21 Evac 17 Died 1 Dest 1 Rem 4 Total 64 // Strength 3809 Wastage 5%	
			OPHTHALMIA Rgt 3 A 1 Total 4 // Cured 1 " 1 " 1 " 1 Rgt 2.	

1-5-18

Army Form C. 2118.

WAR DIARY
or
INTELLIGENCE SUMMARY.
(Erase heading not required.)

Instructions regarding War Diaries and Intelligence Summaries are contained in F. S. Regs., Part II. and the Staff Manual respectively. Title pages will be prepared in manuscript.

Place	Date	Hour	Summary of Events and Information	Remarks and references to Appendices
WARLUS K36d.57 Sheet 51C	13·4·18		Meeting of ADVS XVII Corps & DADVS XV DIV: with Myself in pay Office duty. 'Kercheux'. V.Good. Much improved. Supt 286 Bn RFA. 2/Lieut J.A. +518 Co RE. All satisfactory 35 - Good especially 473 Battery	
	14·4·18		" 2·3·4 Coy ASC. 2·Y·G, 3 Much improved. It then went for improvement. 2/3·W·FA. Very good.	
	15·4·18		" Div HQ. (incl. MMP) Splendid. 1 case of Skin Disease in HD of HQ. Mice: present. Forage acc't.	
	17·4·18		Y·O's meeting in my Office. 19" Routine work with invalids minds. 20" The G+ASC + AC. Very good	
	19·4·18		Returns Rem.t 24. MD 46. Total 69/11 Cured in Care 20. Died 3. Sent to R1 29. Total 69/11 Strength 3346 Mules · 676.	
			Ophthalmia Rem.t 2. A-0. Total 2·11 Cured 1. Cured 0 Remg 1. Y·LT·2.	
	21 "		Visit 40 PDV ETA HQ. I can if there are facilities temporary. Exit myself. As ambulance to Mount in storm. RAPS	
			@ 513 Co RE. Good. 22" to Mobile Sec. with ADVS XVII Re above. Cap. Forrie's Rwrite announc'd Ril	
			Cap. Pilby Lieut. Rade. Good. 24 Warlus Shelled with H.E. GSO I Ic change Billets. 25" Routine work HQ's Medical	
	23 "		Returns Rem.g 24. MD 36. Total 65·11 Cured 14 Evac. to Field Amb. Remg 32. Id 66- Strength 3336 Mules · 496.	
	26 "		Ophthalmia Rem.g 1. Adv. 2. Total 3·11 Cured 0 Evac. - 1 Remg 2. Y·LT·3 26 DDR' Army casting Rumors at Bernaville	
	27 "		Insp M.G. Battalion. Mules. Good. Horses fair. Camp shelled at twilight. 28 Muriel Office Billets - L Nº10 Warlus	
	29 "		Visit with ADVS XVII Corps N°1 CASC. 286-Bn RFA. DAC. 4th A.B. 4D Batts 281 Fld RFA. 168+169 Inf Blds+513 Corps RE.	
	30 "		Routine work with invalids & Specl. Meeting HPO's Re Returns & Home Wounded (Insistency Corps dir.	

1-5-18.

M.Stewart, Maj.
DADVS 56. DIV.

Original

No 27

Confidential
Dear of
S.A.D.S of 56 Queens
S.A.D.S
from 11-5-18 to 12-19-18

Army Form C. 2118.

WAR DIARY
or
INTELLIGENCE SUMMARY.
(Erase heading not required.)

Instructions regarding War Diaries and Intelligence Summaries are contained in F. S. Regs., Part II. and the Staff Manual respectively. Title pages will be prepared in manuscript.

Place	Date	Hour	Summary of Events and Information	Remarks and references to Appendices
WARLUS. K26.d.57. Sheet 51.c.	1.5.18		Meeting of AVC Services in army office for instruction re Returns &c. Inspected ADVS XIII Corps. Div: HQ (Army) + Signals. Insp. with ADVS XVII Corps 575 + 416 Cos RE. 100/281 TM RFA.	
	2/5/18		Insp. with ADVS XVII Corps 575 + 416 Cos RE. 100/281 TM RFA. 21.+ 22/3 THS. His 2.3.+ Cos ASC. 164 Inf Bde + Mobile Vet.	
	3 "		RETURNS. Rewd 32. Attd Inf Vet Offr [?] Cund AV Servs 17 Div 1 Bdr-2 Rewd 55 etd 79 [?] Average 3320 Wastage 4.96	
	4 "		OPHTHALMIA Rewd 2. H.G. Total 11 Cund 4 Was 4 Rewd 3 d/d all 11 Inspected wh ADVS XIII Corps 2/2 London T.A. + 56 M.G. Battalion. Inspected 49 Remounts at BOMYEN	
	5 "		Sundry [?] - heading orders to ASC TMs T.S. Inf. [?] Vet Horses in hospitals [?] ADVS XVII Corps [?]	
	6 "		Met the Ass.g Dy Ins Vety Servs to have and discuss matters with having reference to serving of Cav. Horses [?] [?] in my office. He declines hospital + horse groom + re [?] showing of Hair [?]	
	7 "		Inspected Nos. 3. + 6 Cos ASC + 26 London told Ambs. 9 [?] of T[?] ambus. Albert RD CRIGHTON	
	8 "		AVC (T) arrived Assistance CAPT W + Heaney etched to Nor-vet hosp. to Rev. [?] [?]	
	9 "		Inspected 168 + 169 Inf Bdes cremated 52 G RE with GOC 56 Div. Partners + 2 [?] Ambulance [?]	
	10 "		RETURNS Rewd 38 Ad 39 Total 77 II Cund 23 Cure 19 D'1 Bd 0 Rewd 34. John 14 Total 77 Through 3843 Wastage 5.7%	
	11 "		CAPT W.+ HEANEY AVC arriv. L.N + K VE Hosp. Review for Unit. Meeting at H.Q of ADVS XII Corps	
	12 "		Rev. W + [?] L. 575 + 7 C. RE at WAREUSNIC 14 Divs at HQ 169 inf Bde + 416 C RE at BERNAVILLE	
	15 "		" " 165 Inf Bde at BERNAVILLE 16 " " 167 Inf Bde + 573 Co RE + Bernaville	
	14 "		Meeting of T.Os in Army Offices Omitted Ophthalmia Rewd 3 Ad 6 Total 9 Cund 0 E 2 Rewd 7 Total 9	
	17 "		Insp HA Signals. Tractors gone to Div. 8 [?] OPHTHL Rewd 7 Ad 7 D-H. 11 Cund 0 E 1 Rewd 4 Th.11	
	18 "		RETURNS Rewd 34 Ad 39 Total 73 II Cund 17 E 14 Do 0 D 1 Rewd 41 Total 73 [?] Av 3370 Wastage 4.9% Artillery Conference at H.Q. of ADVS XIII Corps 19. Insp 251 RFA Bde-WC 260 Fd. RFA	

31/5/18 [signature]

Army Form C. 2118.

WAR DIARY
or
INTELLIGENCE SUMMARY.
(Erase heading not required.)

Instructions regarding War Diaries and Intelligence Summaries are contained in F.S. Regs., Part II. and the Staff Manual respectively. Title pages will be prepared in manuscript.

Place	Date	Hour	Summary of Events and Information	Remarks and references to Appendices
WARLUS K36.d.6,7 Sheet 51C	21.5.18		Received 250 All RFA Draft joined Army. Shown to 512 & 416 & for Return unit at DAINVILLE	
	22.5.18		Shown to 168, 116 July Rd. to 612 & 416 & C.RE & BERNEVILLE. No 3 Sw: ISAAC of DAC at MONTENESCOURT	
	23.5.18		Emp HQ & NO1 Sw - 3½ D.A.C at MONTENESCOURT. Y.O.S marching in May HTH - 24 NCO DDR 23 Dmy inf MVS	
	24.5.18		Returns Runy 41 Ad-29 Total 68 // Cand 17 E 16" D 3 D+1 Remy 82 Total 63 // Mount 378 Mach gun - 6 ½	
	25 "		OPTHALMIA. Runy 4 Ad- 1 Total 5 // Cured 0 E 1 Runy 4 Total 5 // Shown to No HQ & Signals of WARLUS	
	26 "		Sup: 513 & C.RE HQ 167 Sup: (Det + Mechanics) at DAINVILLE + M.G. Battn.	
	27 "		Rec application from civil lease from Vic. it & md MVS in mid of serious accident-& his Father.	
	28 "		Gave 3½ lecture to 512 & C.RE 114 Mechanics at DAINVILLE & 116 & C.RE no reason known.	
	29 "		" 168 M.G. Bn Supt Batn & 513 to C.RE at BERNEVILLE	
	30 "		CAPT C W TOWNSEND proceeded on special leave to England to take up KS commission in May 9th	
	31 "		Supt London & Midx Reg 5 + 2½ Indian Field Ambulance	
	"		4 Midx Reg: AT. ITA (including M in P) Signals. Wire to Remts 2 Capts & Lts Lt.H Lebegue	
	"		Returns Runy 32 Ad 24 Total 69 // Cured 12 E 12 D+0 D+1 Rem 34 Total 59 // Mount 2740 Mach gun - 3 ½	
	"		52 " OPTHALMIA. Runy 4 A 3 Total 7 // Cured 2 E 0 Rem 5 Total 4.	

Hy Shecut Major
RAMS 62 Div.

1-6-18

Vol 28

Confidential
War Diary
of
6th Division

BAONS
from June 10th to June 30th

Army Form C. 2118.

WAR DIARY
or
INTELLIGENCE SUMMARY.
(Erase heading not required.)

Instructions regarding War Diaries and Intelligence Summaries are contained in F. S. Regs., Part II. and the Staff Manual respectively. Title pages will be prepared in manuscript.

Place	Date	Hour	Summary of Events and Information	Remarks and references to Appendices
WARLUS K36 d 6.7 Sheet 51C	1-6-16		Insp¹ 169 Inf¹ Bde. 2 Insp 2I.6 Bde + 93/280 RFA 3 Insp DAC ÷ 2.3.+ 4 Co. Div. Train	
	4 "		Lectured to 513ᵗʰ ÷ 416ᵗʰ Coy RE ÷ 164 RFA Establishment - DAINVILLE	
	5 "		To ADVS VII Corps ÷ Vet- Ev. Station to arrange of Strongtite sent by MVS unknown to me. (512=[?]RE)	
	6 "		Re = 6" = FC RE for Stongtite. Thanked no Noncoy carry[?] unstructured unit.	
	7 "		Lectured 168 Hy [?] + Rideo in BERNAVILLE. b Insp¹ 6/13 in M⁹ Bur with G.O.C. V.O's meeting in my	
	8 "		Office. Insp² Removals at MONTENESCOURT. ÷ Insp 167 Inf Bde. ÷ 1st Cheshires.	
	9 "		With DDVS Army ÷ ADVS XVII Corps to 512ᵗʰ ÷ C RE ÷ 1.0 Ldn MVS re Strongtite.	
	10 "		Returns. R⁷ 34 Ad 23 Total 57 || Cured 19 Ev 7 D³ 2 Dyd 2 R⁷ 27 Total 67 || Strength 3793 Horse y c.35	
			Opthalmia R 6 Ad 2 Total 8 || Cured 1 Ev - R⁷ Total 8 || Insp² B ÷ 277 Fd. MFA Westminster	
	11 "		Section Div HQ ÷ Signals. Insp² Removals at Montenescourt. 10 Insps to FC RE ÷ Remounts.	
			Insp: 6/ss, 7/3 Batty ÷ 2/4 AFA Bde ÷ No. 1 Co. 6 ASC. (a Lecture) M⁹ G. Ruston (N3)	
	13 "		Insp 2/1 T/3 + Amb 2 + 13 + C Bhurt 277 AFA Bdes. Inviting NCO's in my Mess	
			Returns. R⁷ 7 AD 28 Total 35 || Cured 10 Ev 9 D³ 3 Dent 2 R⁷ 24 Total 35 || Strength 3602 Horse y c.36	
	14 "		Opthalmia. R⁷ 7 A 5 Total 12 || Cured 3 Ev 1 R⁷ 8 Total 12 || Lectured 1/5 Cheshire Battalion	
	16 "		to 2/4 AFA Bde with ADVS XVII Corps re Strongtite. Sunshine ÷ induced [?] inhalation not Strongtite.	
	17 "		Lecture ÷ MG Coy. Capt CW Townsend RFA Am Leavt (most picket) HLA 7 Army who reported by WO	
	17.19		& confirmed ADVS XVI Corps who inspected all Mr Div Artillery including this DAC.	
	30 "		H No 1 Remount Dept (Morelle) with Brig Gen Coke Will - Remount for him ÷ the GSO I	

30/6/16

[signature] Major DADVS [?] Div.

WAR DIARY
or
INTELLIGENCE SUMMARY.

(Erase heading not required.)

Army Form C. 2118.

Place	Date	Hour	Summary of Events and Information	Remarks and references to Appendices
WARLUS K 26.d.5.7 Sh 51 C	20-6-16 21-6-16		Capt J Hill A.V.C. T.F. attended on 4 days leave to ENGLAND. Coming later. Lieut P.H.C. Roberts 3/4 Army Field Amb. V.O.'s meeting in my office.	
	" "		RETURNS. R 31 A 40 TOTAL 71 Cured 19 Ev 16 D 2 Died R 34 Total 71 Strength 3820 Mules. 4670 (Approx)	
	" "		8 " 7 " 15 " " 5 " 2 " R 9 & Total 15 " 22 Sick 166 " Chinese Battalion	
	28 " "		Cert: mule of the Div: for the purposes of monthly returns. (In accordance with DV'S Circular, memos)	
	30 " "		At a whole the animals are looking very good & better than they have ever looked. It is interesting to note the different routine adopted in feeding by the various units all arriving at the same result. I append a summary of monthly meaning on 1-6-16 to 3 Nor Bde 2 ft 9 f. grease. 13 units. 3 N Bde 3 H.T. A.H.T.G. 4 N H B.T. 2 H.T.G. 11 Units. 4 N H 4 3 H.T.J.G 9 Units 4 N.A.D + 4 H.T.G. 1. 5 N.A. Bde (weighing chaff ac) 1. 5 N.A. D + 2 H.T.G. 2 Units. b.N.A. Bde D + b H.T.J.G. 1 Unit. 9 tried 3 very well... There were returned 4 my Unit, they are very frest used by the 6 N.B.O Bde (Dm chaff)(H T Units) + 5 N.M.D. + S.M. Holf. H.T.G. 2 Mules first is difficult - being too Sudden in the first in the 3 units are little lost - allowed Hindi wheel in often c (N.T. S XIV Corp 3e numeral approx). 21 V.O's meeting in my office. Lieut Mc Girr - 25 " Lieut McGirr on outsit 9 oc. 4 listened 115 Churchies.	
	26 " "		RETURNS R 91 ST AA Total 51 Cured 18 Ev 10 D 3 NoA D R23 Total 51 Strength 377 b Mules. 4 4 70	
	28 " "		Optimum R b A 5 Total 13 Cured 3 Ev 2 R 8 Totals 13 by Lieut-May H.H. + 70 Simmistes	
	29 " "		Re Shipping of Mules - At request of numerical experiments . Lieut Mag.	
	30 " "		Crated mules in May	

30-6-16

R.H.S.R 52 R

19

Confidential
War
Diary
of
D.A.O.V.S. 56th Division
From July 1st 1915 to July 31-1915

Vol 29

Army Form C. 2118.

WAR DIARY
or
INTELLIGENCE SUMMARY.
(Erase heading not required.)

D.A.D.V.S.
56TH DIVISION.

No ....
Date July 1918

Instructions regarding War Diaries and Intelligence Summaries are contained in F. S. Regs., Part II. and the Staff Manual respectively. Title pages will be prepared in manuscript.

Place	Date	Hour	Summary of Events and Information	Remarks and references to Appendices
WARLUS K.39.d.57 Sheet 51 C	1-7-18		So ADVS XIII Corps. He (illegible) 2nd — Inspected May attays D.A.C. RFA & Guigwin Ammunition Park & 5 Canadian DAC. Nothing of importance to report. Returned to HQrs.	
	2 " "		L.M.V.S. for debility & injuries R (not humans L.D) & reported to ADVS XIII Corps.	
	3 " "		Returned H.Q. Auxiliaries arrived at 5" Canadian DAC. V. Group Hy. my attr.	
	4 " "		Returns. R.33 A.22 T.45 (C.11 E.V.10 D – D.Id – R.O.H. T.I.5) Strength 2893 Wastage 30.10	
	5 " "		Ophthalmia. R.3 A.6 T.14 C.3 E.V.2 R.9 T.4 Vaccine MVS hard 2.3 + 4 Cd.ASC	
	6 " "		Inspected 56" Div. Auxiliaries arrived to Brao of Montenescourt & Rant. HuntesBow & Sect. DAC LMVS hard (illegible) Inspected Vet. Supplies. Capt. J. Hill reported & joining Base Remt. Running (illegible) on Ret. H	
	7 " "		Cars arrived from N.B.D.A.C on the 6" inst & sent to be disposed at L.MVS. an Epizootic LYMPHANGITIS Specimen received and examined on June 6" from Boulogne and was neg. HEC on Natural Brud	
	" "		Evented an Awful (illegible) so far 36" Inspected on July 2nd 5 new L.MVS by man on July 15" of M.S.	
	8 " "		Section Commander to Kiker int. Not of Neet Ins. not out VDs Bacteriology. 3" instd L.MVS & identify Remind with ADVS XIII Corps. Visit 1st Anc. B.A.C. It using Mt. Revolution there were no plans of sound	
	" "		Conformed agreed & Visit Inoculator at H.Qr. of Troops. HEC series initially Ye. Note of twould revision, morphine (illegible)	
	9 " "		Note Conference Net. ADVS of Army at L.MVS with ADVS Xth Corps. Insp.Vet.Offic. L.MVS 1st Arth. Sub kims of illness pecing to mouth. Ammo. Oase.	

1-8-18.

P.D.Acott Major DADVS 56 Div

Army Form C. 2118.

WAR DIARY
or
INTELLIGENCE SUMMARY.
(Erase heading not required.)

Instructions regarding War Diaries and Intelligence Summaries are contained in F.S. Regs., Part II. and the Staff Manual respectively. Title pages will be prepared in manuscript.

D.A.D.V.S.
56TH DIVISION.
No ....
Date ....

Place	Date	Hour	Summary of Events and Information	Remarks and references to Appendices
WARLUS Rd A 57 Sheet 57 E	10.7.18 11.7.18		Inspected 1/1 Middlesex. Much improved over last ADVS XIII Corps at Hn.L. Asst. DAC in E.L. Visited DDVS 1st Army & many HAVS XIII Corps at No 1 Sec DHC in E.L. Visited many army HVs	
	12. "		RETURNS. R9.A.23. T.49. C.12. Ev15. D.1. D.5. R.14. T.1. Wastage .56% Strength 3730	
	" "		" " OPTHALMIA R9.A.4. T.13. C.2. Ev.3. R.8. T.3.1. Inspected animals at A.T. D 1/250 1st Cavalry	
	13. "		Inspected 1/6 Div. Signal Co. with G.O.C. Found 3 unsatisfactory animals being replaced with many of	
	" "		the A minimum of A p.tem of Health management. Visited MVS & horses 2/7 A.B. R.F.A. Asc.Co. 1st Office ADVS XVII Corps re Injuries which has been to England. Inspected 1/2 D.A.C.	
	14. "		RVE L " " HA 51st DAC RFA & horse hosp inspected Dress LVs Mule A.E.C. in H.4 Sheet. Field Arty	
	" "		Moved to ROELLECOURT & HORNSN MVs also normally. Returned daily on ADVs XIII Corps at Neuvillette	
Roellecourt T21 d 5.5 Sheet 44 B	15. " 16. "		Moved Army Hy by to BRYAS & CALHUON the this of the ADV Strength at Army 118 including 15 people.	
	17. "		to Corps + MONCHY BRETON. He Arg Inspected & transferring from Rollies which had been 15 people.	
MINGOVAL V23 Central Sheet 44B	18. " 19. "		Moved Is MINGOVAL & Wondin moved to BETHENCOURT D1 A 2 7. Visited 1/5 & 2/7 Corps A.M.V.S.	
	" "		Cap't J R CONCHIE Arrived on short leave to England. Attended conference of DDVS 5th Army. Coming	
	" "		RETURNS R14.A. 16.T20. C.12. Ev.15. D.D.1. R.F. 5. T.3011. Strength 3670 Wastage .35%.	
	20. "		" " OPTHALMIA R8 A.2 T.10.1 C.8 Ev.2. T.10.11. Visited ADVs of 4th Corps of A.T.A. Veterinary R.E.Co.	
			Insp 1/6 Div HQ + Signal Co. Capt W Townsend & 1/1 Londonshire Officers Arrived & took over their ALTS.	

W. Mount M day
A Army 1st 1914

1-9-15

Army Form C. 2118.

WAR DIARY
or
INTELLIGENCE SUMMARY.
(Erase heading not required.)

Instructions regarding War Diaries and Intelligence Summaries are contained in F. S. Regs., Part II. and the Staff Manual respectively. Title pages will be prepared in manuscript.

D.A.D.V.S.
56TH DIVISION.
No ....
Date ....

Place	Date	Hour	Summary of Events and Information	Remarks and references to Appendices
MINGOVAL V.A.3 Central 21.4.18 March 4B			Visited D.D.V.S. & Army H.Q. Capt TOWNSEND R.M.V.E.S. Carried out 217 Corps Evat. No. 36 Vet. [?] Section & M.G. Bn.	
	22 "		30 E. Army Remount Depot. Inspected Remounts for C & O & 4 P.M. 56th Div. Also 6 & 7th Corps Offrs.	
	23 "		to Corps V.E.S. H.Q.S. 24th Inspected 2 G" & 381 D.A.C R.F.A. 26 Field A.M.S. 8th Corps Inspected	
	25 "		An A.J.C. R.E. & 168 Inf Bde at Chateau de la Haie. Visited C.M.V.H.S. L.O.s meeting in my Offr.	
	26 "		Returns R.S.A.D. T.S.H. C & EV 18. D.O.D & R.U.T 66.11 Strength 8649 M.U. Cas.-854.	
	27 "		" OPTHALMIA R. O A.I.T J.I. C & EV. 0 R.1. T.I.I 412 Field Ambulance formed during Annexa...Awarded	
	28 "		Carnation 4 Killed 4 Ev.18 Wounded. 327. M.R.P. horses Killed [Ev W Total	
	29 "		Visited Corps Vet Returns & 458 American Reinf. 25 Insp" 8 & Air to Brigade. R.A.G. & M.G. Battalion	
	30 "		All day (9.30 a.m. to 6.30 p.m.) with 9 & Armentiers Division. Assisting in Administration	
	31 "		3. V.E.S. H.M.S. & 2/3 Field Ambulance 31st V.O.s Meeting in my Office & visited 8th Corps Offrs.	
			Inspected 7 Remounts.	

1-6-18

Pro Lieut
Maj
MAJ & A.D.V.S.

24 WR 30

Confidential —
War Diary
of 56th Division
R.A.P.V.S.
From 1-8-18 To 31-8-18

Army Form C. 2118.

WAR DIARY
or
INTELLIGENCE SUMMARY.
(Erase heading not required.)

Instructions regarding War Diaries and Intelligence Summaries are contained in F.S. Regs., Part II. and the Staff Manual respectively. Title pages will be prepared in manuscript.

Place	Date	Hour	Summary of Events and Information	Remarks and references to Appendices
MINGOVAL V 23 Central Sheet 51aB	1-8-18		Visited 147th Bde RFA 16th Div: an ADVS Corps to investigate cause of an outbreak of Rheumatic articular fever. by Canadian ADVS to Gas. Found 33 cases in A/Bur. 27 in B 9 in C 41 in D 4 in HQ. All cases alike + exception 4 cases situated on the truth of the face. attributed cause to thirties animals had been turned out late in fields covered with much Lucerne and sprouts of turnips. To XVII Corps. Review & inspected Reinforcements for 6th Div at MONTENESCOURT.	
WARLUS K27d 57 Sheet 51c	2-8-16		Moved to WARLUS. MVS to MONTENESCOURT. Returns R11 A47 Total 63 11 Cwt 7 Ev in D 4 Dy's R 30 Total 65 W. Strength 3661 War Equip. 60% OPHTHALMIA. R1. A1 T.2 1 Cwt. – Ev – R – Total 2 1	
	3-8-16		To Corps + then to 177th R.L.A. RFA with DDVS & shewn who interviewed any shoemakers as tennant Attendents	
	4-8-16		To Corps. MVS. 6th L. Corps. Imp 2 " Sect – DAC + 416. The R.E. duty Punished by striking Indian L. Corps + trucks 2 9.8 – Army Bde RFA. Cavalry Bde. D. Division D/Ford. A Te. 6. Int all been sure	
	5-8-16		Ability Cases. Imp. 2 672 = 7. Ca. R.E. Good. 1st to XVII Corps. VE5. No case of sheaf. EL from 75th American Div: Review. MVDSR5 2 Army. 2 Divie. He thinks out EL. Struck it in	
	6-8-18		To XVII Corps. VE5 + 76th American Division to inspect transfer to Veterinary. Re ANZIV bi input of Cavs of Infy dimps. Stomatitis Contry: Int-S.C.	
	9-8-16		Returns R 30 A 29 Total 59 11 Cw 16 Ev 11 D. & A/3 4 R 26 Trans 59 11 W. Strength 3774 War Equip 46% Just over the MADVS 51 Div	

Army Form C. 2118.

WAR DIARY
or
INTELLIGENCE SUMMARY.

(Erase heading not required.)

Instructions regarding War Diaries and Intelligence Summaries are contained in F. S. Regs., Part II. and the Staff Manual respectively. Title pages will be prepared in manuscript.

Place	Date	Hour	Summary of Events and Information	Remarks and references to Appendices
WARLUS K37d57 Sh51C	9-8-18		OPTHALMIA R. A. Total 1 Cui 1 Ev 1 R' Tot 11 Inspected 2/1.F.A.9. 2/2.9. & 2/3 FA.V.9. except showing all Artwich might be improved. ADVS XVII Corps returned from leave.	
	–		LXVII Corps K'handed to LTDVS. LT/VS with DDMS re Surgeons at E.L.	
	10-8-18		Reinspected 282 Army Bde RFA. Conc. & seen from C/Bar & others in Sun. Into W.later	
	11-8-18		Ev: 6 from B/Bar, 3 from A (1 thin) & 3 from D (1 thin) all to Ability. 12" Insp: C1250 QWR (1 thin)	
	12-8-18		Indian Sections YMMP. 13" Insp: DAC (except No 2 Sec) V.9.	
	14.8.18		Insp: 282 Army Bde Am. Col: Fair. Several stain smoken. 15" Meeting at XVII Corps ADVS offie.	
	15-8-18		Re Cupping. LFMVS. 16" M250 Dll RFA hunted. 2 killed 10 wounded. 1 severely	
	16.8.18		Returns. R26 A30 Total 46 11 Cui 12 Ev 9 D – DM 2 R23 Total 46 11. Average 36.96" Wastage 3.70.	
	–		OPTHALMIA R2 A1 Tot.3 11 Cui 2 Cu1 R. – Total 3 11 RAMVS 16 – Div: visited re lichen ova	
	19.		Lt/250 M's animals wounded by bomb. Sh 51C	
LaCauroy N6a7b Sh51C	18"		Moved LECAUROY MVS & DOFFINE FARM C30a6 & Insp' in Ruitz & PERNIN.	
	19"		LTMVS Hunt N2 to Div Train – 22nd Division moved to BAVINCOURT Area. 23rd Division	
	23"		moved to BASSEUX (near H.Q). Sh at LENS 11 – 24" Rear HQ moved to X3d 48 Sh51C.	
BASSEUX X5d78-51c	22nd		Return. R23. A 11 Total 34 11 Cured 11 G.A.Q. Died 1 Sent. 1 Reng 12.11 Strength 3665 – Ophthalmia Nil	
	29"		" R12 A63 Total 75 11 " 4" 9 " 21 " 7 " 34 11 W.E. Juan. May 36.23 – " 1 case Admitted re wrg	
			R.A.M.V.S 17" Ain	

Confidential
War Diary
of
R.H.Q.V.S., 2ᵈ Division
From September 10ᵗʰ 1918
To September 30-1918

Army Form C. 2118.

WAR DIARY
or
INTELLIGENCE SUMMARY.
(Erase heading not required.)

Instructions regarding War Diaries and Intelligence Summaries are contained in F. S. Regs., Part II. and the Staff Manual respectively. Title pages will be prepared in manuscript.

Place	Date	Hour	Summary of Events and Information	Remarks and references to Appendices
BOILEUX S11 a 6.8.(57b)	1-9-18		Moved to BOILEUX. MVS. also moved to BOIRY-ST-MARTIN S15 a 6.4 Alt 11.51 b.	
	6 "		D.A.D.V.S. put from 14 days leave to England. Casualties during September. Sergt. W. Wounded 18	
	" "		Returns R1 34 A 53 T 87 II Cas 14- E 39 D 6. D16. R11 T 571 strength 369 Matdr 2.2 70.	
ARRAS G29 d 64.(57b)	8 "		MVS. Moved to TILLOY. 10th Moved to ARRAS. Capt S. Hill A.V.C. pot'd duty from hospital.	
	11 "		Insp' 280th Bde RFA. A.h. Coy Horse battery slightly emaciated & emaciated pack animals slightly	
	12 "		Insp' 251 Bde RFA all good. 13th Insp' D.A.C. all good. Int'-Shoeing in No 2 section writer.	
	14 "		Insp' MG Bat Good. Also inspected Arm'd Car. Very good.	
	" "		Return R 11 A 69 T 98. II Cured 3 E 23 D 23 Dest 32 R 9 T 72 II strength 3 Ago Wasted 2.1 70.	
	" "		Casualties By shell fire & bomb killed 20. Sept 32 Cured 16.	
	15 "		Insp' R.E. Field Cos. 416-475.13 V.G. 513 Int'-mosquito repellent had ticks & lice and nits.	
LES FOSSES FARM N12 a 6"9 (57b)	16 "		Moved to trees farm N12 a 5.3 (57b) 17th A.D.V.S. as 6tbs visited on premonition	
	" "		Sent in to promotion for a Commission. It GAMBLE LIOTT of the 4th Army M.V.S. left him to	
	18 "		be interviewed at-1st Army HQ. DAVS 1st Army. 13th Visit 168 Infantry V.G. Ins' & Battn	
	" "		transport for exchange other than Brummer Harness. V.O's missing in my opinion	
	" "		Visited Canadian M.G. of Retreat Factory with a view fitting over & Int'-Its Field Hospital	
	19 "		& their harness throughout of a breakdown. Ind. Heavy and good. Otherwise satisfactory	

3019/16

Army Form C. 2118.

WAR DIARY
or
INTELLIGENCE SUMMARY.
(Erase heading not required.)

Instructions regarding War Diaries and Intelligence Summaries are contained in F. S. Regs., Part II. and the Staff Manual respectively. Title pages will be prepared in manuscript.

Place	Date	Hour	Summary of Events and Information	Remarks and references to Appendices
LES FOSSÉS FARM N12a 5,3 (57.D)	20-9-16		Relieve Rems 1 & 3 & 7 & 9/11 Que de 12 E 25 D – Ngl g Reng 24 T 2 9/11 Strength 36 34 Wastage · 9 % Casualties by Gunfire Ord 2/6 O.W. 5. Attended Cookery farm held by R.A.R 1st Army	
	21-9-16		La Cru Corps V.E.S. re reorg. of Sup. Ech L.V.M.P. cmd of AVS’s later attended Mot. Cons. Conf. reinspection hut No 2 Res. D.A.C. from which suspicious eye cases. 23 Insp. 61 Bde. Hpd. but L.R.B. fullen off a little	
	23-9-16		Reconnoitred HAVECOURT V[?] w ARTOIS for MVS Ath. Ecoles Ad. ford-w-VIS w. ARTOIS	
	24-9-16		104 Inf. Bde. horse shows all morning. In 1st Army Remt. Dept. [illegible] charge of the B.S. O1 Y.O. O16.1. Ob.h	
	25-9-16		[illegible] out with the 1st Ry. Rd. re hsc. casualties. 26 Insp. 78 Remounts at R.D.A.C.	
	27-9-16		Return R24 c/67 T9/1 W cure 6 - E 30 D 17 Rests R94 27 T9/1 Strength 3576 Wastage 1.3 % Gun. R bar. Cas. Cas. Died 16 G 12 . 28 Insp. 250 Bde R.F.A. [illegible] Inmates 4 cases.	
			Insp. 3 Field Ambulance all satisfactory. 29 Myself to VILLERS-CAGNICOURT	
VILLERS CAGNICOURT P32 d c 6¼.	30 -''- 30		Visited 255 Bde R.F.A. with ADVS XIIIrd Corps re Inmates	

[signature]
DDVS 5th Div.

30-9-16

WD 33

Confidential
War Diary
of
S.H.Q's 56th Division
& 61st Division
from 1-10-16 to 81-10-16

Original

Army Form C. 2118.

WAR DIARY
or
INTELLIGENCE SUMMARY.
(Erase heading not required.)

Instructions regarding War Diaries and Intelligence Summaries are contained in F. S. Regs., Part II. and the Staff Manual respectively. Title pages will be prepared in manuscript.

Place	Date	Hour	Summary of Events and Information	Remarks and references to Appendices
VILLER'S CAGNICOURT P32 d.A.57.L	1-10-18		1/4 Baradin (London Scottish) transport - three wounded. Casualties 13 killed 5 seriously wounded 3 wounded	
	2.10.18		Having only just moved no transport Reserves concentrated & no shell proof dug outs available 1/2nd MVS moved to V16 in ARTOIS. 2 VO's meeting in my office	
	3.10.18		Returns. R24 A-88 Total 115 Murray Ev 24 D1603 I Rº40 Total 116 HH 1-4 Strength 3603 Wastage 2-8 Addition	
	4 " "		Influenza having practically died out except in remounts which eventually were affected in small numbers	
	5 " "		1st Middlesex transport three wounded casualties 6 killed 8 3 seriously wounded 2 wounded.	
	6 " "		Insp - 250 Bde R.F.A A Bat Fair (3 Ability) D Tric (3 Ability) B pow of complies about 4½ men	
	7 " "		C Much improved - but 4 Altium. B.A.C Fair 1/2 complies 1 Altium 4 men.	
	8 " "		1/4 London MVS moved to CHATEAUX at HENDECOURT. 2nd Imperial MVS Good	
	9 " "		Insp - 250 Bde R.F.A A Int'st(adding) 6 Ability severely 4 minor very thin .	
	10 " "		93 - Good Antgun track a little. C (ten good) D Good (4 thin)	
			Insp - 251 Bde R.F.A A Tric B Good (much imp) 109 very good D Good 11 V sick wastage HORSES 1.3	
			Returns Rº 40 A33 Total 93 II Cured 14 Ev 22 Died Dead 8 Rº95 Total 93 Strength 3505 Wastage MULES 3	
	11 " "		Insp M.G Battalion. Satisfactory. Insp 156 remounts at HENDECOURT	
	12 " "		Insp 114 Reg (Black Scottish) Q. + 115 Reg (Kensingtons) Good. Half-bodied Press drainage of Russell still	

9/11/18

Brevet Maj. DAVIS

WAR DIARY
or
INTELLIGENCE SUMMARY.

Army Form C. 2118.

Place	Date	Hour	Summary of Events and Information	Remarks and references to Appendices
VILLERS CAGNICOURT Road e.11.6/7b	16.10.18		Visited MVS & Canadian Corps ADVS. 16 Mxvd 16 Etrun L3d A14 S16 MVS 16 Anzin G8 L IM1 57 d.	
ETRUN L3 d A1 57 c	17. "		Attended Conference GOC re moving Northwest.	
	18. "		Returns B83 - A at 101 16 M cured 14 Ev 26 Died, Dest 2 R'd 13 11 Strength 3609 Wastage/mean. 58% Mules. 74% horses. Insp 164 Stable It Q. Very good.	
	19. "		Insp 167 Fut Park Ht Q. 2 London Favoured now Hy to town. LR13 YQWR. Very good.	
	20. "		Insp 167 Fut Park Ht Q. 11 London. Strange ? Murdo Perry & ? Mids Pour tw horses not lifted thro Mularghm.	
	"		6 MX Foot escort Riders Ford lrg Visited 10 horses. Can lift, retrained w/ 11 horses Greswicourt. Ambulancy.	
	21. "		Insp 4 Cav RE Ht6 - Gp 512 F 673 G etc m - 2 horses known.	
	22. "		Le Quesnies Cagnicourt - hr hr clearance camp left behind. Still misting.	
	23. "		Insp MG Squadron. Saw 10 cases in team Hut Pennsylvania Amerman. Insp S&A C. Very good.	
	24. "		Insp Dit Q including MMPT depot. VOs meeting at my office.	
	25. "		Returns Rta A 36 Tot 149 11 Cured 6 Ev 15 D 3 Died 1 R'd 24 11 Strength 3681. Wastage horses. 55% Mules. 3%	
	"		Insp 168 Inf Bn. 14 London Fus. Vy Int 3 own Reform. L Sentinel G mustring 3 Kennington G Int 137 hind horses from light.	
	26. "		At MVS of ? Jersey Visited MVS temp Otn. UJ Insp 2 wr div. escort 167 Feld & RFA & NO 6 ASC	
	27. "		Jordan Cagincourt - hrs and horses still Mudymphony. CAPT CREIGHTON on leave to England.	
	28. "		Le Warmquiber revisited L-cn PerbeamPark for Corps march 29 H MVS Can Corps visited my offic.	
	30. "		VO's meeting no my office. Le MVS & remnts ? Middlesex Rennemont Amersp. Change.	

2/11/18

Army Form C. 2118.

WAR DIARY
or
INTELLIGENCE SUMMARY.
(Erase heading not required.)

Instructions regarding War Diaries and Intelligence Summaries are contained in F. S. Regs., Part II. and the Staff Manual respectively. Title pages will be prepared in manuscript.

Place	Date	Hour	Summary of Events and Information	Remarks and references to Appendices
BOUCHAIN BASSEVILLE H.32 B.0.2	31-10-18		Moved to Bouchain. Mrs Hony and Anzin for one day. Stream rich cover throughout. Left behind Returns. Play A To To 39 (Cured 5 Evy Died 1 Reply 14 Strength 26 y 1. Marchy from 2 / o Mules . 470	
	2-11-18		Inspect Mi [illegible] Whites bath	

19 J.U. 34

Confidential
War Diary
of
P.A.D.V.S. 56th Division
From November 1st 1918 to November 30/1918

Original

Army Form C. 2118

WAR DIARY
or
INTELLIGENCE SUMMARY.
(Erase heading not required.)

Instructions regarding War Diaries and Intelligence Summaries are contained in F. S. Regs., Part II. and the Staff Manual respectively. Title pages will be prepared in manuscript.

Place	Date	Hour	Summary of Events and Information	Remarks and references to Appendices
BOUCHAIN (BASSEVILLE) H3d.0.2	1.11.18		MVS moved on 1st to MARQUION & on 2nd to PAVE VALENCIENNES Q.6a.3.0. S41.51A	
SAULTAIN F26b.24.	2 " "		Moved to MONCHAUX J34.a.6.3 M.1.57 & " Moved to " SAULTAIN. F26b.24 S.L-51A	
	4 " "		11 Indn MVS moved to MAING J15.b.6 M1.57 * 5th Lancers the lost Rds. of 51 Field Amb.	
	6 " "		HQ & CARE Red & LD horses & Mules killed by shell fire. MVS moved to SAULTAIN F26b.2.8 M1.57	
	7 " "		Returns R°24 Add° 66deta. 90 || Cured 13 Ev 10 DisDied 2 R130 Strength being Wed.Night 1.10% M 1.1.1%	
	8 " "		Supt of A at Valenciennes. 11 "B" to RASNES M 22 + Capt Cooper V.E.S.	
FAYT LE FRANC B 11.d.10.5. Mont 67	9 " "		Moved to FAYT LE FRANC B11.d.10.5 M1 67. 10 Visited O/C 22 Corps M.T. - Thorpe with DDVS " Army MAYSsal Capt	
	10 " "		Went: MVS moved to FAYT LE FRANC B11.d.10.5. M1.57 11 Armistice signed with Germany	
	11 " "		to QUEAVY LES PETITS en famr 2/1 F.A. Armapot Avilee. 4 H.A. horses burnt 1R+1LD horses kept	
	12 " "		— Visited H.Q. hm i. F.A. 13 to QUEAVY LES GRANDS me 3 horses left behind by m? Div R.F.A.	
	12 " "		Lunch 67 Div M.G. Batt. 16 Chaulnes + 21st Ind. F.A.	
	14 " "		Returns R130 A 47 Died 71 ||Cured 8 Ev 26 - D18 Addd 3 Red ess ||Strength 3637 Wed Nigh H 1-36 M 6%	
	15 " "		V.O's meeting in my office. 16 Lunch NotR 4 Cav. 67 Div Trans. Div. Hd Sigmala.	
	17 " "		Lunch RO Remounts for R.F.A. Impected 25th B. R.F.A. for casting purposes for A.R.O. Ev et 34.	
	18 " "		Lunch ee R.F.A. ditto Cast 53. 7th Middx Regt Cast 4. 20th D.A.C. ditto Cast 23	
	19 " "		Lunch 8. 169 Inf. F Bde. V.O's meeting in my office	
	20 " "		Returns R 28 A = 114 N total 142 || Cured 21 Evac 10 Died 0 Rem 16th th Weznk 3571 Wed nir H3.5 M.6%	
	21 " "			

1.11.18

Army Form C. 2118

WAR DIARY
or
INTELLIGENCE SUMMARY.
(Erase heading not required.)

Instructions regarding War Diaries and Intelligence Summaries are contained in F. S. Regs., Part II. and the Staff Manual respectively. Title pages will be prepared in manuscript.

Place	Date	Hour	Summary of Events and Information	Remarks and references to Appendices
FAMT LE FRANC R.11.d. 10.6 d.51	22-11-18		Insp^t Wil^t 672 4878 ? Us' RE 23 Insp^t 4 London Visited Adv^s camp at 3/3 FA r ADVS 1st Army	
	24		To BOUCHAIN to inspect 274 Remounts which arrived by train to this 1st Bustain WILT D D R 1st Army	
	26		Insp^t 274 Rem^ts (sent) GMVS for Repatriation Scheme (3) PUM(?) Dirty (1) Skin disease (1).	
HARVEING W16.b.2.4 Mar.45	27		Visited new area to which adv: troops MVS 18 March to HARVEING W16.b.2.4. MVS Adv WIG.d.5.9.	
	28		Returgues Rem^t 16 Ad 40 Tot: 55 Cured 9 Ev 32 D3 Dod 4 Rem^t 7 11 Strength 3704 Vach H.6 % M 2.5%	
	29		Reported to A DVS XXII Corps at MONS 30 Inst: XXII Corps hold Surety + transferring in civilian Matters at GIVRY. 18 Ind camp.	

[signature] Lieut. Maj
D.A.D.V.S. 56th Div:

1-12-18

Confidential

WAR DIARY

of

D.A.D.V.S.
4 of 1/1st London M.V.S. 56th Division

From 1 Dec. 1918 to 31 Dec 1918

WAR DIARY
or
INTELLIGENCE SUMMARY.
(Erase heading not required.)

Army Form C. 2118.

Place	Date	Hour	Summary of Events and Information	Remarks and references to Appendices
HARVEINQ	1.12.18		Inspⁿ 2/2 Bonds, F.A. 165 R.A. HQ & No 3 Co Trains & XXII Corps Mounted Troops at HARVEINQ & Subunits	
Wit. A. 21. Map 14S	2 " "		A.D.V.S. XXII Corps visited & Insp^d Mange cases in civilian stables at GIVRY & Il Fords, MVS.	
	3 " "		Inspected DAC & arranged with Butcher at GIVRY to k/t aker all terrain good orst of horses or mules at	
	4 " "		1 franc 25 cent. per Kilo live weight. 4th Anti-Belgian civil V.O. in consultation re Mange at GIVRY.	
	4 " "		Veterinary Captⁿ J. Hill R.A.V.C. TF proceeding to England for 14 days leave.	
	5 " "		V.O.'s Meeting in my office. Visited & Inspected 250 Bde RFA. The King visited this area.	
			Returns R^a y A^a 42 Total HQ || Cured 1 Ev 23 Died 3 Dest 4 R^a 18 || Strength 3836 Week H-78/M. 39%	
	6, 7, 8"		Attended Board Meetings with Major Clarke & Capt Gwynne to shew Board Committee.	
	9.12.16		Inspⁿ M.G. Batt. 1/5th Chesh^s. 10th Inspⁿ 1/2 Lond. 1/5th London & 5/3rd Fd. RE	
	10 " "		Inspⁿ Nw Tbs RE HQ RA HQ & Signal Co. 11 Inspⁿ DAC & No Co Trains & Ett 1/16 London	
	12 " "		Returns R^a 18 A^a 20 TOTAL 38 || Cured 15 || Ev 11 Died 1 Dest 1 R^a 10 || Strength 3438 Week H. 26/M	
			Inspⁿ 4/VII RE 6th Middlesex & No Co Trains. 16th Inspⁿ 147 Bde HQ 1/8 DiV & 7 Middlesex.	
	14 " "		XXII Corps Committee for inspection of hard wares &c arrived around 17 Mears.	
	16 " "		Inspⁿ 1/2 & 1/4 Lond. 18th V.O.'s Meeting in my office.	
	17 " "		Returns R^a 10 A^a 26 Total 36 || Cured 9 Ev 17 Died 1 Dest - R^a 9 || Strength 3410 Week H. 3%, M. 6%	
	19 " "		Visited 18 Fds & 1/1 Lond and H. Butaine R.G.A.	
	20 " "		[signature]	

Army Form C. 2118.

WAR DIARY
or
INTELLIGENCE SUMMARY.

(Erase heading not required.)

Instructions regarding War Diaries and Intelligence Summaries are contained in F. S. Regs., Part II. and the Staff Manual respectively. Title pages will be prepared in manuscript.

Place	Date	Hour	Summary of Events and Information	Remarks and references to Appendices
HARVAN G. WILBY-24 ANT'48	21-12-18		CAPT J R CRICHTON RAVC T. met with accident - thrown from his horse. Had to be had C.C.S. MONS. Hd to take over by me. CAPT C W TOWNSEND doing CAPT J HUNTS work (as been + now reported sick)	
	23-12-18		30 Cavalry Damaged MONS with horses for casting by D.D.V.S. Army 15 horse cast.	
	26- "		RETURNS R 1 q A 12 TOTAL 21 CURED 3 EV 4 DIED 2 DEST 2 R 10 AdmittedA 3729 Treat: H. 4 M. 7	
	27- "		30 CAVALRY BARRACKS MONS with horses for casting by D.D.V.S. Army 3 12 horses cast.	
	28- "		Commenced examining & describing all animals in the division for demobilization + continued daily.	
	31- "		R. V.E.S.s & MVS's. I wish to record my opinion that the former have met them of any advantage whatever to the 61st Div. It has been found necessary to strengthen in France the division to meet the R.A.C. only & M.V.E.S. being as far as my group that much more have been required to meet it. M.V.E.S. shown when we evacuated direct to the base & were then taken from the M.V.S. establishments. In from M.V.E.S.'s, In my opinion the M.V.S. in their normalcy. It never was under the strength within the period in addition to it. Again if new animals were rendered to R. any V.E.S. close enough to	

Major D.A.D.V.S 56 Div

1-1-19

Confidential

War Diary

of

S.A.D.U.S., 56th Division

From January 1st to January 31st 1919

Army Form C. 2118.

WAR DIARY
or
INTELLIGENCE SUMMARY.
(Erase heading not required.)

Instructions regarding War Diaries and Intelligence Summaries are contained in F.S. Regs., Part II. and the Staff Manual respectively. Title pages will be prepared in manuscript.

Place	Date	Hour	Summary of Events and Information	Remarks and references to Appendices
HARVEING W/At 24 M 45	1.1.19		Inspection of Annuals for Classification for demobilization continued daily & V.O.'s Abortrail.	
	2 "		Returns R/10 A 39 Total 49 ||Cured 6 Ev 12 Died 6. R/11 ||Strength 3419 Wast: H 1·32/M 1.1 %	
	3 " "		Escort telemoted under A,B,C,D daily Various units of the division completing the Barum on the 11th January.	
	9 " "		Returns R/11 A 26 Total 87 ||Cured 5 Ev 15 Died – Dest 7 R/11 ||Strength 3685 Wastage Horses 65/Mules 47/0	Sick
	11 " "		18 Horses cast for Relieving Reserve Sold by Public auction at Mons. 18 Lieut B. I. Love. Rays arrived & Relieves Capt. Hill	
	13 " & 14 "		Govt & Classified A B C D & X Y Z 262 Army Bde R.F.A with Capt Townsend Capt Clifford & Statement 282 Classification of division under XYZ for Remounts with Capt Heading & Commenced & Completed on 24th January	
	15 " "		Returns R/11 A 28 Total 39 ||Cured 4 Ev 15 Died – Dest 12 R/9 6 ||Strength Horses 2692 Mules 972 Wast: H 1·27/M 3·2/0	
	16 " "		Sent 18 " Broken Mares away to Mons for Rehabitation. 23 K.O.'s Meeting in My Office.	
	22 " "			
	23 " "		Returns R/9 5 A 67 Total 92 ||Cured 4 Ev 52 Died – 1 Dest 5 R/9 27 ||Strength Horses 2633 Mules 953 Wast: H 1·8/M 1·3/%	Published
	26 " "		Visited HQ 283 Army Bde RFA to inspect American Horses & Mules in Ft. Did not reach Quaregnon but other Mules Vint & Visited No 1 by Corps Horsemasters in XYZ Classification. 27 Visit by ADVS XXII Corps. Mules Hyvorthotin Rum at Villers St Ghislain	
	28 " "		& Reported Sausage estimated at 7pm. 28 Visited D/147 R.E. & Gin R/16 re Sale of Butcher Carts.	
	29 " "		Visited 282 Army Bde RFA re Suspected Glanders case & decided horse was not Glandered as Mallinetin & 3 test	
	30 " "		Reorg. to Mons. We decided & reached by Rail Suntry & Riding 2 Mules & have Arranged & R/C D. A. C. 2.Feb. 1919 W. Ackerr B.DVS First Division	

D. D. & L., London, E.C. (A8004) Wt. W1771/M2731 750,000 5/17 Sch: 52 Forms/C2118/14

Army Form C. 2118.

WAR DIARY
or
INTELLIGENCE SUMMARY.

(Erase heading not required.)

Place	Date	Hour	Summary of Events and Information	Remarks and references to Appendices
HARVEING W166 A.4 ADV4S	30.1.19		K.O's Meeting in my office. Saw Capt Goneine who returned on leave to England on January 23rd — Returns R127 A&30 Total 57 Buried 2 Ev.10 Died Dec 28 R121 Strength: Horses 8104 Mules 904 Wast. H 33% M. 2.42%	
	31 " "		Visit by A.D.V.S. XXII Corps. He asked heavy wind blown down at Mons on the 6th	
	" " "		9.D.2 number of animals destroyed. Fees for burying during the month 64 Munition Reports/32198-25	

[signature] Major,
2 February 1919 D.A.D.V.S., 56th Division.

WS 34

Confidential

War Diary

of

R.H.N.S. 2ⁿᵈ Division

From February 10ᵗʰ 1919
to February 28 19.

WAR DIARY
or
INTELLIGENCE SUMMARY

Army Form C. 2118.

Place	Date	Hour	Summary of Events and Information	Remarks and references to Appendices
HARVEING W 16.c.2.4	2.2.19		Inspected supposed case of mange but no mange by same - unit unknown to civilian at GRENAY. Took precaution. Number left mange in kennels of APM. 3rd Visit by Hon Wardle XXII Corps.	
	3.2.19		F² Field Cashier 15608.15 for Butchery & Sent Consolidated ABCDXYZ Returns to QF Corps.	
	5.2.19		Returns R⁵¹ A⁶⁰ Total 81 ||Cured - Evid|Died|Destᵈ R 27|| Strength:- Horses 2362 Mules 930 Wastage:- Horses 3% Mules 4.3%	
	8.2.19		Visited ADVS XXII Corps re arranging sale. 10⁵ F² Field Cashier 18003.75 for Butchery 11 Arranged Sale at GNR¥ 19 ᵗʰ scale	
	13.2.19		Returns R²⁷ A⁷¹ Total 102 ||Cured 6" Evid Died Destᵈ R¹⁵ ||Strength:- Horses 2654 Mules 1191 Wastage:- Horses 1% Mules 1% Acting	
	15.2.19		To ADVS XXII Corps for Conference with DDVS 1ˢᵗ Army re Sales & to Morís Sale as acting ADVS XXII Corps	
	14.2.19		Entrained 93 horses & 36 Mules for Lille & Hallines || 19 F² Field Cashier 32400 Francs for Butchery.	
	19.2.19		Sold 93 horses at 943.00 Francs - average 10.14 - 36 Mules at 2610.5 - average 7.40. Total 12 out Jan 5 to 6020 Fr.145	
	20.2.19		Returns R 16 A 193 Total 209|| Cured 4 Evid Died - Destᵈ R¹² ||Strength - Horses 2060 Mules 1125 Wast - Horses 29 Mules 6%	
	23.2.19		Inspection of Riding horses to select Infantry Chargers. 24 Galvahing horses & Mules for sale.	
	25.2.19		Visited Grand Remt to arrange Sale for 28ᵗʰ Ide. To move on MHK week	
	26.2.19		Sold by horses at 79750 - average 1156 & 63 Mules at 41450 - average 658 Total 121200. Jan 5030 Commission Francs	
	27.2.19		Returns R¹⁴ A⁶⁶ Total 170||Cured 4 Evid Died - Destᵈ 18 R¹⁰ ||Strength:- Horses 1863 Mules 1089 Wast:- Horses 2% Mules Nil	

M. Scent, Maj
R.A.D.V.S. 1st Div.

2-3-19

Original

~~1/1st London Mobile Veterinary Section~~

DADVS 56th Division

War Diary

March 1919

CONFIDENTIAL.

WAR DIARY

of

D.A.A.G. 56th Division.

From March 1st/1919. To March 31st/1919.

Army Form C. 2118.

WAR DIARY
or
INTELLIGENCE SUMMARY.
(Erase heading not required.)

Instructions regarding War Diaries and Intelligence Summaries are contained in F. S. Regs., Part II. and the Staff Manual respectively. Title pages will be prepared in manuscript.

Place	Date	Hour	Summary of Events and Information	Remarks and references to Appendices
HARVENG	5-3-19		Add 81 Z mules at GIVRY at 90 L50 ft. average 1113 + 447 Z mules at 36 L50 ft average 783.	
W166.2.14 Adrs:—			Total 1370000 lbs 2½ ℔ corn to Animal.	
	7-3-19		Return R10. A 249 Total 305 ¼ Cured 1. Ev 14 Died 1 Dest 83 Sold 2308¼ + Field Cas 213 Horses 1152 Mules 841 Nos+ 291 7½	
	7-3-19		Add at GRAND REWG 72 Z horses at 29790 W: 865 + 302 mules at 20150 average 670 Sold 813 20	
			New 2 ℔ 2½ ℔ LT ℔ Ouctioneers 2032-50. Rd L-Field Cashir 798 L7-50 Depreciation 1200 Mule 600	
	10-3-19		Add at GIVRY 93 Z horses at 4970 av: 1047 + 412 mules 31750 ave 775 Total 13,8950 Less 2½	
			℔ Corn to Auctioneer 3316-75. Rd L-Field Cashier 10,57531-25. Highest Aver 2700 Mule 1350	
	19.3.19		P-Field Cashier 35002-50 to Auction't + 80 animals 1256 W	
	13-3-19		Return Rb A 167 Total 156 Used — Ev — Died 3 Dest 18 Sold 104 Rg 3 Uneuck P-Mm 75 Mules 46 Mu 122 . 2	
			P-Field Cashier ℔1750 Transfer to 19 Animals Sold for distribution	
	20.3.14		Return R3 A13 Total 16 Cd 6 Na Kest 8 Ltd — Rvry 2 Week 3a 562. Horses 1120 Mules 142 Fenst. 712 Inouch	
	24-3-19		P-Field Cashier 3250 for 3 horses sold for Distribution	

24-3-19

(signed) Major,
D.A.D.V.S., 56TH DIVISION.

Army Form C. 2118.

WAR DIARY
or
INTELLIGENCE SUMMARY.
(Erase heading not required.)

Place	Date	Hour	Summary of Events and Information	Remarks and references to Appendices
Hannut	25-3-19		Major Scotts leaves for demobilization to U.K. Capt C.W. Townsend acting D.A.D.V.S. 56 Div.	
	25.3.19		Pour Force Bashir Tas. — 962-50 for 2 animals for Bulkher	
	28.3.19		Returns R. 2 a b. total d. 6t. Add. 3 Nut. 1 R. Total 8.	
	30.3.19		Capt B.W. Townsend leaves for Demobilization to U.K.	
	31-3-19		Capt J.R. Couchie acting D.A.D.V.S. 56 Div.	
	31. 3.19			

(CW Townsend) Cy Major,
acting D.A.D.V.S., 56TH DIVISION.

WAR DIARY or INTELLIGENCE SUMMARY

Army Form C. 2118

STAFF/VS 56 D

Place	Date	Hour	Summary of Events and Information	Remarks and references to Appendices
JEMAPPES (BELGIUM)	1-4-19	-	CAPTAIN R. BRIGHTON R.A.V.C. (T.F.) proceeded to LONDON DIVISION Cttee of Occupation for duty in event of BDDs Func. being No 30/420/V.S. dated 26-3-16 - CAPTAIN C.W. TOWNSEND R.A.V.C. T.F. proceeded to U.K. for demobilisation. - CAPTAIN J.R. CONCHIE R.A.V.C. T.F. takes over as Executive V.O. of 56t Brigade Group and Actg. D.A.D.V.S.	
"	6-4-19	-	Return - Nil Sick Strength of animals - Owners - ress 45 Horses and 36 Mules Total 81. Remounts Untraceable personnel R.A.V.C. as Divisional suggested to Control 2mg 3 pr. Mobilization leaving now only Cadre "A" of M.V.S. viz. 2 V.O.S (Captn. J.R. CONCHIE R.A.V.C T.F.) and LIEUT B.J. LOVE R.A.V.C. (T.C.)	
"	9-4-19	-	Orders received for departure of LIEUT. B.J. LOVE R.A.V.C. T.C. by almost. Strength 146 Horses + 36 Mules total 181	
"	10-4-19	-	Return. No sick.	
"	14-4-19	-	All Vet. Kit M.V.S. cable + equipment handed over to the Bn. In accordance together with clar. copies of Cbard Mobilzn the Table A.F.W1078-79 under auth of 3rd Divn. Q. authority No.Do: AQX 150/28/10 dated 7-4-19 and in accordance with Stand. Regulations Goes Animals are Mules + two Horses sold to British Local Market having authority having under to Hand. Ze proceeds 1512 fra 50c. handed on to Field Cashier an 14-4-19.	
"	16-4-19	-	LIEUT. B.J. LOVE R.A.V.C. entered hospital sick	
"	17-4-19	-	Strength 143 Horses 37 Mules Total 78	
"	19-4-19	-	Admitted 2 Destroyed 3. One Horse of MMP destroyed and sold in Lottery. Le proceeds 500 Francs Cash to Field Cashier XIII Corps on 21-4-19	
"	24-4-19	-	Returns admitted 1 Destroyed. Strength 142 Horses 35 Mules Total 74	
"	27-4-19	-	One Horse 3rd Bttn. and one Mule 1/6th R.B. destroyed sold in Lottery. Proceeds 940 Francs paid to Field Cashier XIII Corps on 29-4-19	
"	29-4-19	-	Capt. J.R. CONCHIE R.A.V.C. (T.F.) proceed to U.K. on duct of demobilisation	
"	30-4-19	-	The only remaining R.A.V.C. personnel in the Division are the 7 O.R's in Cadre of 1st Lond. M.V.S. at Wasdale.	

Winterton Col.
D.A.D.V.S., 56TH DIVISION

www.ingramcontent.com/pod-product-compliance
Lightning Source LLC
Chambersburg PA
CBHW081435160426
43193CB00013B/2286